"I first met Christine during a silent retreat at the Notre Dame Retreat House, when she presented me with a copy of her book, *God's Love Illuminated*. The spirit I felt through her devotionals gave me solace, reassurance—and the deep sense that God was speaking to me through Christine's words. Her book changed my spiritual trajectory and helped me identify my inner aches and illuminated the path I should follow moving forward. I am looking forward to reading Christine's new book, *God's Grace Manifested*, in hopes it continues to guide me as I walk the path that was revealed. I genuinely recommend this book—and anything else Christine writes. Because the truth is: Christine does not write these books. She is the instrument. It is the Holy Spirit who moves through her when those words find the page. I believe that if you open your heart, God's grace will surely enter—through Christine's words."

Larry Alfonso Villasmil Urdaneta
Associate Professor, P.E., Rochester Institute of Technology
Rochester, NY

I0540745

"Much like sprinkles on an ice cream cone, grace decorates the ordinary moments of our lives. I'm not sure I have met anyone more alert and attuned to the channel of God's gifts than Christine. In all of her books, Christine joyfully shares the rich flavors of her experiences. The stories in this book, *God's Grace Manifested*, will encourage you to begin your own daily search for grace. With her gift for connecting scripture to her personal journey, Christine invites readers to uncover similar patterns in their own lives and notice the sacred 'thin' places that surround them. Each reflection includes thoughtful questions that deepen prayer and draw readers into a more intimate relationship with our generous and loving God. Take time to savor the sprinkles."

Meg Castellini
Director of the Spiritual Renewal Center
Syracuse, NY

"Few souls understand what God would accomplish in them
if they were to abandon themselves entirely to Him and if they
were to allow His grace to mold them accordingly."
~ St. Ignatius of Loyola

"God's grace is often easy to recognize in religious services and formal prayers. We expect to see and experience God in those areas of our lives. But what about those most ordinary of moments in life? Christine gives us a wonderful aid to our growth in holiness and abandon to God through her reflections filled with authenticity and the sharing of divine love. May these reflections inspire all to more easily recognize God's grace being manifested in their daily lives."

Jodie Scordo
Assistant Director at the Notre Dame Retreat House
Canandaigua, NY

"What is life really about? How can we get the most out of it? Is it about seeking happiness or inner peace? Why is there so much hurt going on in the world? These questions are best answered in the spiritual realm. This word, 'spiritual,' has taken on much importance in recent generations as so many are often saying, 'I am spiritual, but not religious.'

"There are many definitions of spirituality:

a method of arriving at union with the Divine.

a conversion of heart.

a journey to the Center.

an integration of life on a deep level.

an education of the heart.

managing the human condition in terms of the Ultimate.

"Christine Fisher would never negate the fact that she is religious, but she certainly is highly spiritual, and she shares her spiritual journey through ordinary and practical, smooth and easily readable events of daily life. This book clearly articulates the way in which Grace, God's life within us, answers the four questions above."

Fr. Robert Thomas Werth
St. Frances Xavier Cabrini Parish
Rochester, NY

"When I met Christine Fisher, I entered into the infectious excitement of her love for God and seeking His presence through His creation. She shared pictures of how He showed His love for her with heart-shapes embedded in wood or in flecks of crystals in gray stones, a heart-shaped cloud poised over a blue lake, and three cross shaped contrails bisecting each other in a clear sky. Even heart-shaped flecks of mustard on a napkin! Christine was authentic and genuine, and her powers of observation were amazing! It made me wonder what signs from God I may have missed because of my lack of focus. The reflections within this book will amaze you and perhaps you will wonder the same thing and have your eyes opened to see more of God in the ordinary."

Karen Batsford

GOD'S GRACE MANIFESTED

MANIFESTED

Treasured Thoughts to Inspire Life in Abundance

A 90-DAY DEVOTIONAL

CHRISTINE M. FISHER

God's Grace Manifested
Treasured Thoughts to Inspire Life in Abundance
Christine M. Fisher

To contact the author:
christine@hopetoinspireyou.com
www.hopetoinspireyou.com

Published by:

Mary Ethel

Mary Ethel Eckard
Frisco, Texas

Library of Congress Control Number: 2025925033
ISBN (Print): 978-1-966561-32-3
ISBN (E-book): 978-1-966561-33-0

Cover photo by Christine M. Fisher, 2024
Location: Brown Hill Farms, Tunkhannock, PA

CONTENTS

SECTION 2: GOD'S GRACE MANIFESTED THROUGH THE SPIRIT

SECTION 3: GOD'S GRACE MANIFESTED
THROUGH PEOPLE..**201**

SECTION 4: GOD'S GRACE MANIFESTED THROUGH THE FOOTSTEPS OF ST. PAUL

DEDICATION

I dedicate to God this labor of love that fills me with joy as I witness the gift of grace that is manifested in our lives. It is a free gift from our Creator that we need to extend to others.

My heart is filled with gratitude to God for allowing me the gift of writing as the avenue to best process my faith and share with others. I have discovered that writing is like giving away the few loaves and fishes one has, trusting that they will multiply in the giving—blessing others and myself at the same time.

This book is also in appreciation for all those who throughout the last eleven years have read my weekly reflections on my website, hopetoinspireyou.com, and inspired me to share some in book form.

And, last but not least, I dedicate this book to my mom, Gail, who for many years has edited my weekly reflections and books. Thank you for your tireless work to make it all come together and sound even better.

I love you all dearly and appreciate the gift you are in my life as we journey in faith.

"Grace and peace to you from God our Father and the Lord Jesus Christ. I thank my God every time I remember you. In all my prayers for all of you, I always pray with joy because of your partnership in the gospel from the first day until now, being confident of this, that he who began a good work in you will carry it on to completion until the day of Christ Jesus."
~ Philippians 1:2-6

FOREWORD

Some things take time to grow.

This seems to be the lesson that the Lord has been showing me lately as I have introspectively looked back on my life. It rings true in the area of friendships, especially with my precious friend, Christine.

I have never been one to bare my soul all at once and have always considered myself an introvert. Small talk and speaking with people I do not know well are difficult for me, but I have adapted over the years out of necessity. People who know me would probably say I am an "extroverted introvert," because I have spent a lot of energy trying to be something I am not—which is being an extrovert!

The seeds of my friendship with Christine go back almost twenty years to when our young sons were in the same class in a Christian school in upstate New York. Because the class size was so small, it allowed the kids (and their parents) to come together for many elementary school events and class parties. It was a close-knit environment which made getting to know people easier. For a few years, our relationship centered around these school events, along with an occasional play date with our sons. Slowly but surely our friendship began to grow and take root.

God's grace is perfectly timed.

It wasn't until a few years later, with my husband's passing, that our relationship reached a much deeper level and truly solidified. Many people in my life, although kind and supportive, seemed to avoid my pain after this sad event. But Christine was different; she leaned into my hurt and offered her listening ear and loving embrace when I needed it most. She was a steady, constant source of comfort during that difficult stretch of life. Isn't that similar to how God loves us? He always leans into our pain and hurt, and His love and grace fill those broken places in our hearts if we allow Him to. I was broken. My heart was shattered, yet I still heard God whisper, *"My grace is sufficient for you, for my power is made perfect in weakness." (2 Corinthians 12:9).*

As the roots of our friendship grew deeper still, I began to see a reflection of myself in Christine. I am someone who desires connection but sometimes struggles to connect. Christine had shared that she wrestles with the same thing at times. We were both introverts, and also seemed to be drawn to the helpless, the hopeless and the unseen. Christine regularly volunteered at the local NICU and held the tiniest souls in her loving arms. She looked at this as a ministry, and although these babies would never remember her, she knew they needed to be held and loved and prayed for in those first weeks of life. Just like me, she often befriended elders and seniors, forming deep and lasting friendships with many of them. Over time these similarities became more apparent. Is it possible that God put us together on this earth to show us something about ourselves, or even something greater than ourselves?

With God there are no coincidences.

One afternoon while Christine was at my house, she glanced through a family history album that my father-in-law had completed and given to me. After turning a few pages, Christine noticed her own family name in the genealogy. To both of our amazements, we quickly discovered that we are cousins through marriage! Who could orchestrate this other than God? It made me think about Christine's favorite verse, *"And we know that God works all things together for the good of those who love Him, who are called according to his purpose" (Romans 8:28).*

Growing through God's grace.

I began thinking about the concept of God's grace. We know we can be changed in an instant, in a single act of grace, when we accept Christ's forgiveness and salvation. But we have also been given the gift of His grace throughout our lives, as imperfect humans, to rely on day to day. I was left pondering one of the quotes in Christine's newest book, *God's Grace Manifested.* It reads, *"God's grace provides for us as we grow in trust toward being who we are meant to be."* Could it be true that learning and experiencing God's grace takes a lifetime?

I've learned that good things do take time to grow and bloom. Perhaps God intends it to be that way. My friendship with Christine is a perfect example of this, as good things are always worth the wait. I have been inspired by Christine's demonstration of quiet courage, and her overcoming personal challenges to allow God to work through her. May we all strive to have that same trust and faith in our lives. My prayer is that we will continue our journey together through this lifetime to grow and become the women God intended us to be.

Carol Palmiter
Sister in Christ

INTRODUCTION

"And the Word became flesh and dwelt among us, and we have seen his
glory, glory as of the only Son from the Father, full of grace and truth.
(John bore witness about him, and cried out, 'This was he of whom I said,
"He who comes after me ranks before me, because he was before me."')
For from his fullness we have all received, grace upon grace. For the law
was given through Moses; grace and truth came through Jesus Christ."
~ John 1:14-17 (ESV)

The theme of God's grace has been resonating in my life. Have you stopped to reflect on the truth that God's grace is always manifested in every aspect of our lives?

God's grace is the unmerited favor and love that cannot be earned that He bestows upon humanity.

God's grace is nothing other than the Divine self-communication in love.

God's grace often enhances the unique abilities and inclinations He has given us to share with others.

God's grace provides for us as we grow toward being who we are meant to be as we grow in trust.

God's grace should move from our ears to the depth of our hearts.

God's grace is sharing or participation in the life of God that is communicated by the Holy Spirit so we might establish and maintain the right relationship with Him and others.

God's grace is the invisible workings of Him that can be understood by the things we touch, feel, and experience that helps understand the Creator better.

God's grace is that which starts, sustains, and completes His work in us.

God's grace is an encounter with His presence often seen in retrospect.

God's grace is the love of God for us given unconditionally and always.

God's grace can be found through the simple joys of life, through the Spirit always at work, in each person we encounter, and through the footsteps of St. Paul. God's grace always has an effect on our lives. May these reflections remind you of the ways you encounter God's grace manifested in your faith journey. All of the ending verses contain a form of the word "grace."

God's grace manifested.

"The grace of God knows no limit or measure."
~ St. Teresa of Avila

Section 1

GOD'S GRACE MANIFESTED THROUGH THE SIMPLE JOYS OF LIFE

"And God is able to make all grace abound to you, so that having all sufficiency in all things at all times, you may abound in every good work."
~ 2 Corinthians 9:8 (ESV)

God assures us that He alone is the one who makes all grace abound in all aspects of our lives. This grace provides everything we need and is always sufficient for whatever situation we encounter. The good that we are able to do is because of His grace.

God's grace is found in the simple joys of life—like a glorious sunrise or sunset, chatting with a friend over coffee, holding the hand of someone near death, or holding a little one close.

God's grace manifested through the simple joys of life.

"The will of God will never take you where the grace of God cannot sustain you."
~ Billy Graham

1

Solar Eclipse

It was a grace-filled experience to have witnessed the total solar eclipse that occurred on April 8, 2024, at Lake Ontario. It was a sacred moment in time that made me marvel at the God of the universe who made the heavens and the earth.

At first the sun was shining, then clouds rolled in, and the sky got darker. But just in time, God graced us with the ability to see the eclipse clearly as the clouds moved from where the sun was.

Around 3:20 p.m., the sky became darker and darker. On the water's horizon, we could see sunlight followed by darkness in the sky above. I noticed how, despite the darkness, there was still light present. The water was still, and we could hear the birds chirping, confused by the darkness.

As the time of totality approached, from 3:22 p.m. to 3:25 p.m., we were in awe of witnessing the beauty of the solar eclipse. Looking at the moon progressing to cover the sun, we could see the outer area, a ring, of the sun's light.

I reflected on how significant it was that this solar eclipse was happening close to the Easter Triduum and Easter Sunday we celebrated a few days earlier.

Consider what happens during a solar eclipse: darkness (the moon) slowly covers the light (the sun). This darkness in our area lasted about three minutes and forty seconds before the darkness, the moon moved away, leaving the light, the sun, to shine brightly again.

The solar eclipse reminded me of Jesus' body on the cross. Darkness filled the earth when He died. What happened three days later? Jesus, the true light of this world, was resurrected. The stone was rolled away, and the light filled the earth.

I was reminded of different parallels between witnessing this solar eclipse and Jesus' life and death.

When, a little after 3 p.m., it became as dark as night, I thought of Good Friday when Jesus died on the cross for you and me.

> *"Even the revolutionaries who were crucified with him ridiculed him in the same way. At noon, darkness fell across the whole land until three o'clock. At about three o'clock, Jesus called out with a loud voice, 'Eli, Eli, lema sabachthani?' which means 'My God, my God, why have you abandoned me?'"*
> ~ Matthew 27:44-46 (NLT)

What a great parallel that the total eclipse happened around the same time of day that Jesus breathed His last. In the last three hours of Jesus' life, the earth became dark for about three minutes.

Observing the stillness and quietness of the water reminded me of how Jesus calms the storms in our lives.

> *"'Lord, help!' they cried in their trouble, and he saved them from their distress. He calmed the storm to a whisper and stilled the waves. What a blessing was that stillness as he brought them safely into harbor! Let them praise the Lord for his great love and for the wonderful things he has done for them."*
> ~ Psalm 107:28-31 (NLT)

What a beautiful psalm to remind us that whenever we are going through a storm or are in distress, we only need to call out to Jesus for help. Our spirits can be as calm as the water was when we cry out in faith to Jesus. He brings us to safety.

The birds reminded me to sing praises to our Creator.

> *"The birds of the sky nest by the waters; they sing among the branches."*
> ~ Psalm 104:12

I love to see the birds flying about near bodies of water. It is even more beautiful to hear them sing praises to our Creator. What a good reminder to try and be more like them, to be carefree, and to sing praises.

As the moon covered the sun, there was a ring of white light that reminded me of Jesus shining in our lives.

> *"When Jesus spoke again to the people, he said, 'I am the light of the world. Whoever follows me will never walk in darkness, but will have the light of life.'"*
> ~ John 8:12

Jesus is the light of the world. If we believe in and follow Jesus, we have His light shining through us into the world and the lives of others. What a wonderful gift. Despite the dark sky, a ring of light from the sun shone forth, being greater than the darkness of the moon. The same is true in our lives.

Seeing the moon continue moving upward until the sun was once again fully revealed reminded me of Jesus' resurrection.

> *"There was a violent earthquake, for an angel of the Lord came down from heaven and, going to the tomb, rolled back the stone and sat on it. His appearance was like lightning, and his clothes were white as*

snow. The guards were so afraid of him that they shook and became like dead men. The angel said to the women, 'Do not be afraid, for I know that you are looking for Jesus, who was crucified. He is not here; he has risen, just as he said. Come and see the place where he lay.'"
~ Matthew 28:2-6

Imagine a violent earthquake followed by an angel rolling back the stone from the dark tomb. The angel was like a brilliant light, with clothes that were bright and white. Though the guards and women were frightened, they learned the good news of Jesus' resurrection.

Remember, life and its struggles may get very dark at times,
>BUT with Jesus, the Son,
>>we always have the victory!
>>>Even in the darkest of times,
>>>>light will return!

A few hours after the eclipse I was in awe of seeing the water look like a stairway to heaven; it looked like the ripples were horizontal and even had vertical ones on each side. I have to think it was some phenomenon of the solar eclipse.

Be encouraged to…

    be present with Jesus in your darkness.

    cry out to Jesus to bring calm and stillness to the storms in your life.

    imitate the birds of the sky and sing continual praises to God.

    share the light of Jesus that shines in you.

    let the power of Jesus' resurrection dispel the darkness in you.

REFLECTION:

What storm can you ask the Lord to help calm?
What concrete way can you share the light of Jesus with someone?

> *"When he [Barnabas] arrived and saw what the grace of*
> *God had done, he was glad and encouraged them all to*
> *remain true to the Lord with all their hearts."*
> ~ Acts 11:23

Christine M. Fisher

2

Our Journeys

I recently participated in two artistic events: Painting and Cake Decorating.

Before the painting class began, one instructor was tracing a sloth on canvases for a future class. I went over and jokingly said, *"I think you should trace all the canvases"* as I explained my apprehension with painting well.

When the instructor began, he said to relax, he would walk us through everything, and he would help if we needed. I started struggling about a third of the way through when another instructor helped me get back on track. He also encouraged us by three statements that resonated with me and are applicable to our lives.

EVERYONE'S PAINTING WILL BE A LITTLE DIFFERENT, AND THAT IS OKAY.

> *"And yet, O Lord, you are our Father. We are*
> *the clay, and you are the potter.*
> *We all are formed by your hand."*
> ~ Isaiah 64:8 (NLT)

Our awesome God created each person to be unique and special, formed in His image—a masterpiece! We are like clay in the hands of the potter, creating a unique, beautiful, and different piece of pottery each time. Our task is to embrace our own uniqueness and beauty just as we marvel at the paintings that we create.

WHEN YOU LOOK AT THE PAINTING ON THE WALL, YOU WILL NOT NOTICE ALL THE IMPERFECTIONS THAT YOU MIGHT SEE UP CLOSE.

*"We are made right with God by placing our faith in Jesus Christ.
And this is true for everyone who believes, no matter who we are.
For everyone has sinned; we all fall short of God's glorious standard.
Yet God, in his grace, freely makes us right in his sight. He did this
through Christ Jesus when he freed us from the penalty for our sins."*
~ Romans 3:22-24 (NLT)

God designed us to be perfectly imperfect, and there is beauty in that. When Christ Jesus died on the cross, His blood washed away the sin that is part of our humanity. Through God's grace in the plan of redemption, God sees us as spotless, like perfection, just like our view of the painting on the wall!

THIS PAINTING EXPERIENCE WAS MORE ABOUT ENJOYING THE JOURNEY THAN FOCUSING ON THE DESTINATION.

*"You make known to me the path of life; in your presence there is
fullness of joy; at your right hand are pleasures forevermore."*
~ Psalm 16:11 (ESV)

We have assurance that God is leading each of our individual journeys. We should value each day's journey, every opportunity that comes along, live in the moment, and not wish our lives away. We can experience the joy of the Lord as He leads us in our individual paths while enjoying the pleasures of His presence and others. With this painting, we were to take time and enjoy the experience—the journey of creating our masterpiece.

The other artistic project was to frost and decorate a cake. I tried to apply the same points from the painting class. I was pleasantly surprised on writing a cursive "Love" on my cake including a few heart shapes. No, it wasn't perfect because the frosting was getting too warm by the time I finished. But I did it knowing the journey was more important as I continued my baby steps of growth.

Be encouraged to…

> accept how God made you—beautiful and unique—different from anyone else.
> know we are all perfectly imperfect.
> enjoy the journey of life each day while heading for the final destination of eternal life.

REFLECTION:

Which one of the three statements do you need to improve upon the most? What perfectly imperfect trait can you surrender to God?

"Not that I have already obtained this or am already perfect, but I press on to make it my own, because Christ Jesus has made me his own."
~ Philippians 3:12 (ESV)

3

You Never Know

It has been an honor that three out of my four books have been nominated for the Henri Award in Christian Literature. Self-publishing the books has been a grand adventure with God.

When I went to Texas in 2023 to attend my first Christian Literary Awards where *God's Love Illuminated* won the Henri Award, my publisher sat next to me. It was a beautiful evening from start to finish.

In 2025, we met for the fourth time as she and her husband accompanied me to the Christian Literary Awards gala event. Afterward, my publisher's husband asked to pray with me. He prayed in thanksgiving for my ministry and for continued blessings upon it. Words flowed from my mouth in prayer too. Then, my publisher said something that has stuck with me ever since, *"You think you were here for the awards, but you never know how God will use you."*

Later, it occurred to me how that same sentiment rang true with our first encounter in New York. She thought she was there to share a message, and neither of us knew that a little over a year later, she would be publishing my first book.

"One day as Jesus was walking along the shore of the Sea of Galilee, he saw two brothers—Simon, also called Peter, and Andrew—throwing a net into the water, for they fished for a living. Jesus called out to them, 'Come, follow me, and I will show you how to fish for people!' And they left their nets at once and followed him. A little farther up the shore he saw two other brothers, James and John, sitting in a boat with their father,

Zebedee, repairing their nets. And he called them to come, too. They
immediately followed him, leaving the boat and their father behind."
~ Matthew 4:18-22 (NLT)

Think about Simon, Andrew, James, and John waking up that day and doing what they've always done—fished for their living. They thought that day, like every other day, would be spent earning wages to provide for their family. Jesus had other plans for them, starting that very day. He was calling them to fish for men—to share the good news of Jesus with others so they could repent and have eternal life. Do we drop everything to heed Jesus' call in our lives?

My publisher's statement made me stop and see a few cases of "you never know" from the trip and afterwards which I wouldn't have seen otherwise.

I shared a book with a pastor while waiting for my hotel shuttle after arriving at the airport in Texas. On the second leg of my journey, we sat next to each other on an airport shuttle where I overhead him talking with another man. Since our paths crossed again, I asked if he would appreciate a book. He mentioned that someone at his church had written some stories, which he encouraged her to put into book form. Maybe God's plan is for my book to provide that inspiration for her.

As I was waiting for the hotel shuttle to take me to the airport, there was a couple with a young girl blocking the door as they were verbally fighting. The clerk asked them to go outside, where there was shouting for at least twenty more minutes. It broke my heart to see this little girl sitting there, listening to and seeing this. I prayed for them all and continued for a few days. I trust that my prayers helped the situation, especially the little girl who was led off by the hand with the man—maybe that is why it happened right then.

My plans to meet with a friend didn't work out. Instead, I was able to attend a service where I felt inclined to share a book with a new-to-the-church family. Perhaps God wanted me to be at that service in order to share the good news through the book with them.

Be encouraged this week to...

> be flexible in your plans, knowing God is in charge.
> marvel at how God's plans play out in your life.
> see the importance of the ordinary events where God is at work.
> allow God to use you for His glory.

REFLECTION:

When did you see God's plan that was different from yours?
Who did God put in your path that ministered to you?

> *"But grow in the grace and knowledge of our Lord and Savior Jesus Christ. To him be glory both now and forever! Amen."*
> ~ 2 Peter 3:18

4

Constantly Evolving

How easily do you accept change in your life? Do you resist it? The saying, *"Everything changes"* has always bothered me. I prefer the saying, *"If it ain't broke, don't fix it!"* I am learning to stop resisting change and be more accepting of it, knowing it is a natural part of life and tends to bring goodness.

God made basically everything on this earth to change. Can you see the goodness that comes with the changes?

Consider nature, which goes through the four seasons every year.

> With nature, we can see the beauty of each season and the renewal it brings. The trees progress from bareness to buds, green leaves, to finally multicolored leaves before falling and returning to the earth. We can experience different events or sports in each season, each offering us something special.

Consider the daily changes in the sky caused by weather patterns and even the sun and moon.

> We can see the sun and moon go through their different phases daily, producing beauty. We get to experience hot, sunny days to cold, snowy days and everything in between.

Consider plants and crops.

> We can see the fruit of our labor as we plant seeds, water and fertilize them, and then see them grow into food that we can eat.

Consider the ocean tides.

What a glorious sight to see the ocean waters ebb and flow, sharing beauty that we can be immersed in.

Consider the butterflies.

A mere caterpillar goes through growth and transformation and grows into a beautiful butterfly.

Maybe through all these changes, God is showing us how we, too, need to be constantly evolving to grow into the people He has planned. If we don't change or try new things, there is no growth. As we grow, we can learn and experience more adventures as we strive to be more Christ-like.

"Look around you. Everything changes.
Everything on this earth is in a continuous state of evolving,
refining, improving, adapting, enhancing, and changing.
You were not put on this earth to remain stagnant."
~ Dr. Steve Maraboli

Being more of an introvert, I'm reserved in a crowd and prefer sharing one-on-one. God has been showing me, though, that I need to let go of those preconceived ideas of myself, knowing that He wants us to be constantly evolving into who He created us to be. We should not place limitations on ourselves. Being open to God, with His Spirit leading and guiding us, we can do things we think we can't.

I saw the ripple effect of God's orchestrations that led me to attend a special church service. As I walked in, a lady approached me and said, *"How would you like to do a reading? We don't have any lectors."* I said, *"I have never lectored at a service."* She said, *"You did it in the Holy Land."* Despite the few thoughts that immediately came to mind, like "You can't do this," I felt like I had to give it my best shot. I laughed when she said, *"In fact, you*

Christine M. Fisher

can do two readings." I replied, "I guess it's baptism by fire!" I did not even have time to read through the Scriptures beforehand.

I felt the need for some prayerful support, so I texted a few people minutes before the service started. One person said, "Remember you're doing it for God." Knowing people were praying was comforting and encouraging.

I felt God's presence and peace come over me as I read, despite fumbling over a few words. I was able to look up, read at a good pace, and use expression. Joy welled up in me that I was able to proclaim the Word, which came from my heart.

It is important that we constantly evolve, especially in our faith journey. Don't we sometimes get stuck in our routines and then maybe stop evolving?

> "The Lord gave another message to Jeremiah. He said, 'Go down to the potter's shop, and I will speak to you there.' So I did as he told me and found the potter working at his wheel. But the jar he was making did not turn out as he had hoped, so he crushed it into a lump of clay again and started over. Then the Lord gave me this message: 'O Israel, can I not do to you as this potter has done to his clay? As the clay is in the potter's hand, so are you in my hand.'"
>
> ~ Jeremiah 18:1-6 (NLT)

The Lord is constantly molding and fashioning us into the people He wants us to be. We need to surrender our will and let Him direct our path. Sometimes God has to keep molding us, as we might rebel at first or get off the path. We are assured that we are always in God's hand.

When God calls us to something, He equips us. Do you feel sometimes that you are not able to serve in some way because you are not gifted appropriately?

*"Now may the God of peace, who through the blood of the eternal
covenant brought back from the dead our Lord Jesus, that great
Shepherd of the sheep, equip you with everything good for doing
his will, and may he work in us what is pleasing to him, through
Jesus Christ, to whom be glory for ever and ever. Amen."*
~ Hebrews 13:20-21

God provides us with what we need as we follow His will. We do not rely
on our own power and strength; rather, it is His Spirit working. God is
able to do wonders when our hearts are willing to serve Him and step out
in faith. We can take comfort in knowing God qualifies those He calls.

May you be reminded of the importance of growing in your faith journey
as God stretches you to constantly evolve into the person He intends you
to be. With growth we can do more than we ever expected because God
is working in us.

Be encouraged to…

remember God made things to change and evolve.
be open to constantly evolving and growing in faith.
let God mold and fashion you.
know God equips you with what you need to do His will.

REFLECTION:

What ministry did God stretch you to be involved in?
What is the most difficult change you have encountered?

*"You are the most handsome of all. Gracious words stream from your lips.
God himself has blessed you forever."*
~ Psalm 45:2 (NLT)

5

Unconditional Love

A deacon friend was preparing his thoughts to minister at the nursing home that houses dementia and Alzheimer's patients when, suddenly, God ministered to him. He looked to the courtyard and saw a couple in their 80's holding hands. The husband came every day to visit his wife. He felt he was "witnessing true love." *"What a beautiful example of unconditional love. As soon as he leaves, she won't even know that he was here."* He continued, *"At this moment, I am truly witnessing God's love and compassion, as two hands are locked together, so peaceful. It's like time has stopped."* The scene replayed several times in his mind throughout the day. It made me think about our relationship with God.

How many times does our Lord show us examples of true, unconditional love daily and we miss it?

In the...

> fresh start of each day.
> person who encourages us when we need it.
> kindness of a stranger.
> one who is patient with us when we are not being the best version of ourselves.
> friend who listens intently.
> children seen caring for aging parents.

"Understand, therefore, that the Lord your God is indeed God. He is the faithful God who keeps his covenant for a thousand generations and lavishes his unfailing love on those who love him and obey his commands."
~ Deuteronomy 7:9 (NLT)

God is love, and He is faithful from the beginning of time until the end. He loves us unconditionally, even when we don't think we deserve it.

How many times do we fail to take the time to open our eyes to take in God's beauty despite our Lord always being present?

God's beauty found in…

> the gentle rain.
> seeing the perfect Scripture passage that spoke to your heart when you needed it.
> the innocence of a child.
> a parent taking care of their physically challenged child with love and patience.
> the phases of the sky—night, day, sun, and moon.
> someone sincerely saying, *"I love you."*

> *"One thing I ask from the Lord, this only do I seek: that I may dwell in the house of the Lord all the days of my life, to gaze on the beauty of the Lord and to seek him in his temple."*
> ~ Psalm 27:4

May we seek the Lord daily, dwelling with Him and seeing His beauty everywhere we go. May our heart's desire be to see the Lord's beauty in everyone we encounter.

I challenge you to daily identify at least one way you experience...

God's true, unconditional love.
God's beauty.

You are special.
You are God's.
And forever unwearied will His love be for you!

If you live as if you believe that
you are special
and
God's love will never tire,
how will your days be different?

Live in the grace of God's unconditional love as you see His beauty all around you.

REFLECTION:

When have you experienced God's unconditional love most intensely?
What unconditional love act have you witnessed?

"The Lord passed in front of Moses, calling out, 'Yahweh!
The Lord! The God of compassion and mercy! I am slow to
anger and filled with unfailing love and faithfulness.'"
~ Exodus 34:6 (NLT)

6

Savor Life

Let's start with an interactive reflection. Do you have a life saver or hard candy handy? Before you do anything with that life saver or hard candy, let me ask you a question.

> When you have a life saver or some other hard candy, do you savor it for a few minutes before you bite and chew it? Or do you savor it until it's gone?

Interesting to think about, isn't it?

If you are in the first category, is that how you handle life? Do you rush through each day marking things off your to do list, not really savoring each moment?

> Or are you the type that does take life, one step at a time, no matter what, savoring the moment?
>> Do you, like me, need a little reminder to slow down and savor life?

Through the years, I have improved slightly in this area. I now have adult children so there is less constant responsibility in caring for them. But I still have room for improvement, especially since I am a planner. I want to make sure everything gets done timely, with the best outcome and as successfully as possible.

There is great truth in the saying that *"We are never promised tomorrow."* We never know when something catastrophic will happen, so it is important to savor life.

This point was driven home to me for two reasons. One was in attending an unexpected funeral for a young man who was the brother of one of my "adopted sons." His young life was cut short by an accident.

The other was because my daughter, away at grad school, came home for the first time in over six months. Trying to savor each moment, even just listening to her talk, seemed fitting for the short amount of time she was home—just being; not necessarily doing.

How often do we take even the little things for granted as we are rushing around trying to balance everything in this life?

Yes, we have work, the kids, church, sports, extra-curricular activities, family to visit, and God time.

> *"Taste and see that the Lord is good. Oh, the joys*
> *of those who take refuge in him!"*
> ~ Psalm 34:8 (NLT)

How beneficial it is when we slow down, taste, and see how good the Lord is. We are safe and secure with Him. We can see the beauty He has filled this earth with. And we can see His greatest of creation—you and me. He fills all the needs we may have.

What are some ways we can savor life?

When you see the people around you, think about how they are God's creation too—how much God loves them; that He died for them. Treat them with respect and say a silent prayer for them.

In whatever situation you are in, look for ways to be Christ's hands and feet to others—to shine His Light. It can be as simple as waiting to hold the door open for someone, picking up something that someone dropped, offering a smile and friendly *"hello"* to someone walking by.

When you are running around, observe the beauty of creation that is all around you—the hills, valleys, trees, flowers, bodies of water, sky, sunrises/sunsets, a butterfly trying to land on a bush. Thank the Lord for His radiant display of His handiwork.

Take time to really listen to the person you are with—let them explain themselves without interrupting or pushing your views on them. Just be there, accepting their thoughts and feelings even if you don't necessarily agree. Your presence can be a blessing for helping them to savor life.

Keep trying to focus on the current activity you are engaged in—not thinking about the next thing you need to do. Instead of always looking forward to an upcoming event, ask God to help you maintain focus and savor life one step at a time.

May your goal be to savor the moments you are living.

And each time you have a life saver, may it be another reminder to savor life a little more.

REFLECTION:

How has the Lord called you to savor life more?
What helps you to remember to savor the moment?

"But we do see Jesus, who was made lower than the angels for a little while, now crowned with glory and honor because he suffered death, so that by the grace of God he might taste death for everyone."
~ Hebrews 2:9

Christine M. Fisher

7

The Creator's Gifts

God, the Creator of
> everything and everyone
> > in this world,
> > > is the BEST GIFT-GIVER ever!

God's first gift to us was this world and all of creation that is in it.

> *"For through him God created everything in the heavenly realms*
> *and on earth. He made the things we can see and the things we*
> *can't see—such as thrones, kingdoms, rulers, and authorities in the*
> *unseen world. Everything was created through him and for him. He*
> *existed before anything else, and he holds all creation together."*
> ~ Colossians 1:16-17 (NLT)

God created the heavens, the earth, and everything in them: the sun and the moon, the light, the waters, the dry land, the vegetation, the birds, and the livestock, to name a few. He filled the earth with everything good, each in their own way giving praise and glory to Him.

God's next gift was making mankind in His image.

> *"Then God said, 'Let us make mankind in our image, in our likeness, so*
> *that they may rule over the fish in the sea and the birds in the sky, over*
> *the livestock and all the wild animals, and over all the creatures that*
> *move along the ground.' So God created mankind in his own image, in*
> *the image of God he created them; male and female he created them."*
> ~ Genesis 1:26-27

*"Then the Lord God formed a man [Adam] from the dust
of the ground and breathed into his nostrils the breath
of life, and the man became a living being."*
~ Genesis 2:7

God breathed His breath into Adam, and every human after him bears the breath of God. You are made in God's image. Have you considered what a gift you are? In turn, our lives are our gift to God. Does the way you live reflect that?

God gives us both human and spiritual gifts every day.

HUMAN GIFTS

"Ears to hear and eyes to see—both are gifts from the Lord."
~ Proverbs 20:12 (NLT)

*"So if there is any encouragement in Christ, any comfort
from love, any participation in the Spirit, any affection and
sympathy, complete my joy by being of the same mind, having
the same love, being in full accord and of one mind."*
~ Philippians 2:1-2 (ESV)

We are blessed to receive gifts that we experience in our humanity. Some of God's gifts are our sight to behold His beautiful creation, our ears to hear the birds singing their praises, and the friends we can share His goodness with.

SPIRITUAL GIFTS

*"God has given each of you a gift from his great variety of spiritual gifts.
Use them well to serve one another. Do you have the gift of speaking?
Then speak as though God himself were speaking through you. Do you*

*have the gift of helping others? Do it with all the strength and energy that
God supplies. Then everything you do will bring glory to God through
Jesus Christ. All glory and power to him forever and ever! Amen."*
~ 1 Peter 4:10-11 (NLT)

When God created us, he made each of us unique with our own set of spiritual gifts to help build up the Body of Christ. It gives our lives meaning and purpose while we await spending eternity in heaven. The way we use our spiritual gifts is our gift to God.

While taking in the sights, sounds, and beauty of a waterfall, I thought about the truth of something I heard:

We should love the Creator more than the creation.

I stood in awe being in the presence of the Creator gazing on the waterfall. Though the beauty of the waterfall and scenery was amazing, our Creator is even more awesome. God is greater than any of His great masterpieces.

How can we love the Creator more than the creation and the gifts He has given us?

Keeping in mind that everything is a gift from God.

*"You are worthy, our Lord and God, to receive glory and
honor and power, for you created all things, and by your
will they were created and have their being."*
~ Revelation 4:11

Everything on this earth is a gift of love from God. He created everything to fulfill His purposes. Because He has given us everything that is a gift, God deserves all glory and honor.

Living with the awareness that God is in control of everything.

*"I know the greatness of the Lord—that our Lord is greater than
any other god. The Lord does whatever pleases him throughout
all heaven and earth, and on the seas and in their depths."*
~ Psalm 135:5-6 (NLT)

God is in control of everything. What comfort it brings us knowing everyone and everything is in His capable hands. Nothing can compare to the wisdom or splendor that God has.

Continually lifting our voice in praise of the Creator.

*"Praise the Lord. Praise God in his sanctuary; praise him in his
mighty heavens. Praise him for his acts of power; praise him for his
surpassing greatness. Praise him with the sounding of the trumpet,
praise him with the harp and lyre, praise him with timbrel and
dancing, praise him with the strings and pipe, praise him with
the clash of cymbals, praise him with resounding cymbals. Let
everything that has breath praise the Lord. Praise the Lord."*
~ Psalm 150:1-6

As we see both the human and spiritual gifts that God has given us, we will grow in awe and wonder of Him. The Creator's glory fills the world, and He deserves our continual praise.

Be encouraged to praise God, the Creator, for...

being the best gift-giver.
all of creation.
making us in His image.
the human gifts He gives us.
giving us our own unique spiritual gifts.

being the awesome Creator.

being in control of everything.

And be reminded to love the Creator more than any of His creation.

REFLECTION:

Can you name two spiritual gifts God has given you?

What human gift can you give praise to the Creator for?

> *"Each of you should use whatever gift you have received to serve others, as faithful stewards of God's grace in its various forms."*
>
> ~ 1 Peter 4:10

8

Droplets

How many times do we think the little things we do aren't important? How often do we feel we don't make a difference in life?

Consider some little acts of love and kindness like...

> holding a door open for a stranger.
> saying a friendly hello to the person in the hallway.
> taking a few minutes to call a widow.
> making cookies for the new family in the neighborhood.
> thanking the leader of your small group.
> sharing how someone's life impacts yours.

How do these little acts of love and kindness affect your life?

> Let's consider that each of those little things is represented by a droplet of water. As you keep doing more little things for more people, your droplets begin to form a puddle. Sharing more of God's goodness, love, kindness, forgiveness, and compassion makes the puddle turn into a stream. Day by day, as you continue touching more lives, the stream will become like a river. Soon God will turn your droplets into a flood, which is a flood of His love that you want to keep sharing with everyone. It becomes a way of life.

How do these acts of love and kindness affect the recipient's life?

> One by one, in those acts of kindness, the droplets of water from different people in their life will form a puddle. As they receive

more kindness, their puddle will grow into a stream, and then into a river, as they will be flooded with God's love.

One by one, people's hearts will be changed, both the giver and the receiver. We will see the magnitude, depth, and power of God's love. He works through us all, making His presence and love known and felt by so many.

> *"When the dew was gone, thin flakes like frost on the ground appeared on the desert floor. When the Israelites saw it, they said to each other, 'What is it?' For they did not know what it was. Moses said to them, 'It is the bread the Lord has given you to eat.'"*
> ~ Exodus 16:14-15

> *"The Israelites ate manna forty years, until they came to a land that was settled; they ate manna until they reached the border of Canaan."*
> ~ Exodus 16:35

When the Israelites were wandering in the desert for forty years, daily God provided just the right amount of food for them called manna. God made the little turn into enough to sustain the Israelites for forty years, one day at a time.

> *"When the sunshine of loving kindness*
> *meets the raindrops of suffering,*
> *the rainbow of compassion arises."*
> ~ Clive Holmes

A deacon who ministers at a nursing home sent me a text that relates to the little things we do. *"One of the aides just came up to me and said, 'I was sitting around the corner, taking a break, and texting. But I started to listen to what you were saying, and I texted my friend, I hope you have a nice day.' I listened to your words about simple kindness. Thank you."*

We never know how God will use our words or actions to grow those droplets into bigger blessings for His glory.

"The King will reply, 'Truly I tell you, whatever you did for one of the least of these brothers and sisters of mine, you did for me.'"
~ Matthew 25:40

Any act of love and kindness we do for someone is also done unto the Lord. Do you see Christ's face in all your brothers and sisters?

Be encouraged to remember…

that little is big unto the Lord.
that God turns our little droplets into rivers.
to be faithful in the little.
that God produces the harvest in our lives.
that God is working through you.
to sow seeds of God's love.

REFLECTION:

How did someone go out of their way to assist you?
When did you hear that something you did created a ripple effect?

"My son, do not let wisdom and understanding out of your sight, preserve sound judgment and discretion; they will be life for you, an ornament to grace your neck."
~ Proverbs 3:21-22

9

Enjoy the Now

My mind is always busy thinking, planning, reflecting, or racing in many different directions. I have made progress trying to just "enjoy the now," the gift that "the now" is.

My daughter and I drove her car with 350 pounds of luggage, including her two saxophones, cross-country from New York State to El Paso, Texas, as she was beginning her three-year military band assignment there. The trip was 2,200 miles and 32 hours with no traffic or stops. We had six days to get there, and I was excited to be flying back home.

How did I just "enjoy the now?"

> Had no plans on how far we would go each day.
>> Arranged no hotel reservations or stops.
>>> Soaked in the beauty of the scenery as it unfolded—from the lush green mountains and hills to the barren, brown desert area with smaller bushes.
> Praised the Lord for all of His amazing creation.
>> Reminded myself that life is not so much about the destination as it is the journey itself.
>>> Spent quality time praying for others throughout the times of silence.
> Immersed in God's peace and presence while on the open highways.
>> Expressed gratitude knowing God was leading, guiding, and protecting, especially through the prayers of many.

Assurance that trusting the Lord would provide what we needed if and when we needed it.

This was my first trip where we had no daily plans as we drove. We wanted to go as far as we could the first few days to make sure we allowed for any issues that might arise.

This trek goes down in history as the one where I packed the least amount of luggage. It felt freeing to "go light" and to practice living in "the now," one moment at a time, as we drove on the open road. I was reminded of this passage:

"Then Jesus said to his disciples: 'Therefore I tell you, do not worry about your life, what you will eat; or about your body, what you will wear. For life is more than food, and the body more than clothes. Consider the ravens: They do not sow or reap, they have no storeroom or barn; yet God feeds them. And how much more valuable you are than birds! Who of you by worrying can add a single hour to your life?'"
~ Luke 12:22-25

Jesus does not want us to live in fear or anxiety—something easier said than done, I know. But we do need to grow in trust, knowing He is in control. He made the birds of the air and lilies of the fields. Have you looked in wonder and awe at them and thought about how God works everything out for our good? Even when things don't go our way, our faith reinforces that God is with us, providing all we need.

The first day was nice being on some familiar roads of New York State, Pennsylvania, and a few in Ohio. We stopped every few hours, and the time passed rather quickly as we chatted away. Before we knew it, eleven hours were down, and we stopped for the night in Terre Haute, Indiana. Even better for me, my daughter was in charge of picking out the hotels and places to eat while I drove. Being decision free for most of the time was a plus, allowing me more time to "enjoy the now."

Christine M. Fisher

I enjoy driving the open roads, especially the highways, which were 95% of this trip. There was hardly any traffic congestion and not many construction areas. How I love to see God's beautiful creation while driving: the sky, clouds, trees, hills, lush fields, and wildflowers.

The second day we stopped in St. Louis, Missouri, to walk around and to ride the huge Ferris wheel. We were time sensitive because of the instruments being in the hot car.

We stopped in Tulsa, Oklahoma for two nights since we were more than halfway to El Paso. The Oklahoma aquarium was awesome despite the puffer fish (my daughter's favorite) being in quarantine because of the other fish hurting him. We also took in an art museum and garden in Tulsa.

Ironically, it seemed the third and fourth days of our travels, though the shortest amount of time, seemed like the longer drives. We arrived in El Paso on our fifth day, the fourth day of driving. A fun fact is that we drove from one end to the other of five of the states we drove through—Ohio, Indiana, Illinois, Missouri, and Oklahoma, which had some of the most desolate places. It was a little scary, but I would say, *"Jesus, I trust in thee."* It always made me smile when I would see a highway sign with that saying on it, a heart or two reminding me of His love, and even a sign that said, "You are braver than you believe."

Be encouraged to...

> live life to the fullest by "enjoying the now" of each task.
> see the opportunities God orchestrates as you live in the moment.
> know you are more valuable to God than the birds of the air.
> have more faith than worry.
> seek God's peace and presence even in the difficulties.
> know you can do all things with Christ leading.

REFLECTION:

What is one thing that helps you "enjoy the now"?
When did you "enjoy the now" even though it was a difficult season?

> *"May the grace of the Lord Jesus be with you.*
> *My love to all of you in Christ Jesus."*
> ~ 1 Corinthians 16:23-24 (NLT)

Christine M. Fisher

10

Sea Foam

Someone said, *"You need to walk the beach in the rain."* I decided to take that advice and started my stroll during a light rain. While walking along the shoreline with the warm water engulfing my feet, the desolate beach was peaceful.

On my morning walks, the white sea foam washing up on the shore caught my attention. Sometimes the wind would start blowing some sections of the foam together, making it tumble and roll along the sand quickly.

While doing a little research on sea foam, I found it occurs when dissolved organic matter in the ocean, such as salt, algae, and other pollutants, is churned up. When the ocean is agitated by the wind and waves, sea foam is produced to a greater degree.

I see parallels between us and sea foam. The sea foam represents our lives. The Holy Spirit represents the wind and the waves in our lives that produce peace and beauty even during the storms. We need to join with others, represented by the clumps of foam that formed together, rolling as one, as we share our lives with others. We journey together, helping each other through both the rough and calm waters of life.

"Then we will no longer be infants, tossed back and forth by the waves, and blown here and there by every wind of teaching and by the cunning and craftiness of people in their deceitful scheming. Instead, speaking the truth in love, we will grow to become in every respect the mature body of him who is the head, that is, Christ. From him the

whole body, joined and held together by every supporting ligament,
grows and builds itself up in love, as each part does its work."
~ Ephesians 4:14-16

As we mature in our faith, we glean more wisdom from the Holy Spirit about living in the truth of God's Word and not getting caught up in the wrong path of truth. We can withstand the wind and waves that try to take us off the right course. Christ is the head of all and the foundation of our lives. We are each a special part of His body and are joined with Him as we work together to build up and share His love with each other.

Be encouraged to…

> seek the Holy Spirit's gifts of peace and beauty in the storms.
> join with those in your path to help each other navigate the waters.
> share your gifts to build up the Body of Christ.

REFLECTION:

What beauty has God made from the wind and waves in your life?
Who is God showing you to help through the rough waters?

> *"May the Lord bless you and protect you. May the*
> *Lord smile on you and be gracious to you."*
> ~ Numbers 6:24-25 (NLT)

11

The God of Surprises

At a retreat, one of the exercises was to break into small groups and answer the question, "What has surprised you so far?" It was interesting to hear the variety of answers. God made each of us different and unique, so we have different perspectives, usually based on the experiences we've had, and it is fun to hear stories from others. I was proud that I spoke up in our small group too, sharing how God surprised me with the relationships I formed in less than twenty-four hours. I didn't go into detail, but I shared a book with a presenter the first night before I heard him speak. It was a little inkling I had to share instead of waiting until the next day.

The question echoed in my mind for a while, which made me think about how we never know what God will orchestrate in our lives. The next day I was surprised to see the presenter had the book with him as we went into the chapel before heading to breakfast. He told me he had already read some. It was a lovely surprise when he sat at my table, and we had a blessed encounter sharing similar stories. He shared how perfect God's orchestration was for this moment in time and shared a few more sacred encounters throughout the retreat.

The next morning, I heard the birds singing at 6 a.m. and hopped out of bed, thinking I should go see the sunrise. Eventually I headed to the kitchen for breakfast. God surprised me with having the presenter walk into the dining area as I was finishing my food. He sent me off with a powerful blessing and prayer, which was the perfect ending to the weekend.

Another surprise was seeing the lady in the room next to me. As we talked, we remembered sharing some of our stories and realized we had met at this same place three years earlier. What a blessed surprise to reconnect.

> *"'My thoughts are nothing like your thoughts,' says the Lord. 'And my ways are far beyond anything you could imagine. For just as the heavens are higher than the earth, so my ways are higher than your ways and my thoughts higher than your thoughts.'"*
> ~ Isaiah 55:8-9 (NLT)

This verse supports the idea that God is a God of surprises. We tend to think in more human ways that we have control over so much, but God is the true orchestrator. God is omniscient and is the Creator of the heavens and earth and everything that is in them. His mind is way above ours, and He knows how everything fits together.

Does it surprise you that…

God chose Moses, a stutterer, to speak to the Israelites?
Abraham and Sarah conceived a child in their old age, John the Baptist, who would baptize Jesus?
Jesus was conceived by the Holy Spirit and born of a virgin?
Jesus ate with sinners and prostitutes?
Peter denied knowing Jesus three times, yet he was the rock upon which Jesus started the church?
God sent His only Son, Jesus, to die and rise from the dead to save us from our sins?

Be encouraged to…

see what surprises God sends your way.
be in awe and wonder at God's orchestrations.

Christine M. Fisher

be filled with joy knowing God works in and through ordinary men and women.

REFLECTION:

What surprise has God provided in your life recently?
Have you seen how God has worked through ordinary you?

"The grace of our Lord was poured out on me abundantly,
along with the faith and love that are in Christ Jesus."
~ 1 Timothy 1:14

12

Living or Life

*"We make a living
by what we get,
but we make a life
by what we give."*
~ Winston Churchill

What a thought-provoking, inspiring quote.

Do you

make a living…

or

make a life…

with your existence and limited time on earth?

We, like Jesus, live in both our humanity and the spiritual world. Jesus was both human and divine, and we, too, share that because we are filled with the Holy Spirit.

What does make a living mean?

It refers to how we earn money to live. We make a living to meet our physical needs, like shelter, food, and even leisurely activities.

What does make a life mean?

It refers to even more than just making money to survive. When we make a life, it includes both our worldly and spiritual experiences. In

Christine M. Fisher

what ways do we give to others? Do we share God's love and goodness and help others?

"WE MAKE A LIVING BY WHAT WE GET."

We have necessities that need to be provided in this physical world for our survival. Things like nutrients to sustain our bodies, some kind of shelter to protect us from the elements, and transportation that allows us to get places. All these things require money.

> *"Then God blessed the seventh day and made it holy, because on it he rested from all the work of creating that he had done."*
> ~ Genesis 2:3

> *"The Lord God took the man and put him in the Garden of Eden to work it and take care of it."*
> ~ Genesis 2:15

> *"Work brings profit, but mere talk leads to poverty!"*
> ~ Proverbs 14:23 (NLT)

"Work" has existed since the very beginning, when God created the world. He considered it work, and I have to think that for Him, it was a labor of love. We have all of creation where we can see God's love at its finest. Keep in mind that God's prize creation is you and me, as we are made in His image.

Adam, the first man God created, was put in the Garden of Eden to work and take care of it. We, too, join in this work as we tend to the garden of our lives as we use the special gifts and talents God has given us. Our work provides for ourselves and others.

"Whatever you do, work at it with all your heart, as working for the Lord, not for human masters, since you know that you will receive an inheritance from the Lord as a reward. It is the Lord Christ you are serving."
~ Colossians 3:23-24

Whatever work we do throughout our lives, whether we are paid or give of our time, all we do should be done unto the Lord. The way we work glorifies God, the Creator of everything. All that we do is a gift to God.

"WE MAKE A LIFE BY WHAT WE GIVE."

This part of the quote relates more to the spiritual world that we are already a part of. We make the best life when we give ourselves totally to the service of others as we use our time, talents, and treasures to love, serve, and help others.

"Then Jesus said to his host, 'When you give a luncheon or dinner, do not invite your friends, your brothers or sisters, your relatives, or your rich neighbors; if you do, they may invite you back and so you will be repaid. But when you give a banquet, invite the poor, the crippled, the lame, the blind, and you will be blessed. Although they cannot repay you, you will be repaid at the resurrection of the righteous.'"
~ Luke 14:12-14

Jesus tells us the importance of giving to those who have nothing. We need to attend to the needs of the most destitute people. Our lives are enriched by helping those who cannot repay us. Our reward might not be in this world, but at the resurrection, God will acknowledge the goodness we have shown because of our love for Him.

"Command them to do good, to be rich in good deeds, and to be generous and willing to share. In this way they will lay up

treasure for themselves as a firm foundation for the coming age,
so that they may take hold of the life that is truly life."
~ 1 Timothy 6:18-19

This passage encourages us to continually give to others. We are told the ultimate blessings will come when we are in heaven. Each day, there are opportunities to build more treasure with the reward we will reap in eternity as we are open to being generous and to sharing with others.

Jesus' life on earth, especially His three years of public ministry, exemplifies *"making a life by what He gave."* The Bible only mentions that Jesus was possibly a carpenter like Joseph. We then learn more about the work Jesus really came to do, which started when He was thirty years old. He gave continually to others, meeting people where they were, forgiving their sins, healing their physical and emotional ailments, and setting them free from bondage. Jesus' life was one of constant giving and helping others. His ultimate gift to all of humanity was the giving of His very self on the cross.

What are some ways we can *"make a life by giving?"*

> Volunteer at a soup kitchen.
> Evangelize to someone who needs to hear the good news.
> Be there to support and encourage a friend battling health issues.
> Fill a ministry need at church.
> Visit a shut-in.
> Give our treasure to help a homeless person.

Be encouraged to…

> give your best at whatever work you do.
> strive to focus on *"making a life of giving."*

REFLECTION:

Do you need to put your heart more into your work?
In what new way can you live out giving?

> *"Timothy, guard what has been entrusted to your care. Turn*
> *away from godless chatter and the opposing ideas of what is*
> *falsely called knowledge, which some have professed and in so*
> *doing have departed from the faith. Grace be with you all."*
> ~ 1 Timothy 6:20-21

13

Focus

"You can focus on what's missing from your life, or you can focus on the blessings that already exist in this moment."
~ Panache Desai

Isn't it easy to focus on something that is missing in your life?

> Maybe your children moved away as they began their adult lives.
> Maybe you are unable to perform certain household repairs because of the natural aging process.
> Maybe you can't do the ministries you are used to because of physical limitations.
> Maybe the program you thought you were supposed to be involved in did not work out.

Isn't it more important, especially when you feel something is missing, that you change your mind set to focus on the blessings that already exist? An attitude of gratitude can help us dwell on the blessings that we have in our lives rather than focus on what is missing. Isn't that what God wants us to do?

"Always be joyful. Never stop praying. Be thankful in all circumstances, for this is God's will for you who belong to Christ Jesus."
~ 1 Thessalonians 5:16-18 (NLT)

God wants us to be joyful. We can be joyful in times of adversity because we know God is bigger than our circumstances. Joy is not dependent on our circumstances. We are told to pray and be thankful in all circumstances because of Jesus in our lives. That provides encouragement for us to focus on the blessings that God provides rather than to focus on what we think is missing.

> *"We demolish arguments and every pretension that sets itself up against the knowledge of God, and we take captive every thought to make it obedient to Christ."*
> ~ 2 Corinthians 10:5

What we focus on is important. Our focus should be on being obedient to Christ and His word, which gives us the direction and wisdom we need to focus on the most important things.

What blessings can you focus on that already exist instead of having your focus on the above mentioned missing things?

> Focus on seeing those in your life who are like family to you.
> Focus on coming to terms with the fact that everything has a season and a time.
> Focus on finding the form of ministry you can do. It might be calling someone weekly to let them you know you care.
> Focus on trusting that the Lord's will is being carried out in your life, not necessarily your will.

Be encouraged knowing that…

> your life is in God's hands.
> God's plan is sovereign.
> you can trust God is working through all your circumstances.
> God provides what you need when you need it.
> God's purposes will be fulfilled in and through your life, not necessarily yours.
> the blessings outweigh the losses in your life.

REFLECTION:

In what situation were you able to change your negative focus to a positive one?

What is the latest blessing you thanked God for?

"May God be gracious to us and bless us and make his face shine on us—"
 ~ Psalm 67:1

14

Verbal Sunshine

"Be generous with encouragement.
It is verbal sunshine.
It warms hearts,
costs nothing,
and enriches lives."
~ Nicky Gumbel

What is encouragement? If we look at the word "encouragement," we see the root word is "courage," which in Latin is "cor," and is the word heart. A Google definition from Oxford Languages defines "encouragement" as: "the action of giving someone support, confidence, or hope."

Putting all that together, encouragement is giving a part of our hearts to another as we act to give support, confidence, or hope to someone. We share a little piece of our hearts with someone when we offer encouragement.

"But since we belong to the day, let us be sober, putting on faith and love as a breastplate, and the hope of salvation as a helmet. For God did not appoint us to suffer wrath but to receive salvation through our Lord Jesus Christ. He died for us so that, whether we are awake or asleep, we may live together with him. Therefore encourage one another and build each other up, just as in fact you are doing."
~ 1 Thessalonians 5:8-11

We are children of the day meaning of the light, which is Jesus. He is the light that came into this world showing us the way to faith, love, and hope. Jesus died for you and me so we may live forever, in unity with Him. We get to walk hand-in-hand with each other sharing this good news and encouraging one another on this spiritual journey. We get to share our hearts with each other, our hearts full of love and God's goodness supporting, helping others be confident in their journey, and bringing hope. Our lives are overflowing with this so we can be generous in offering encouragement.

What is verbal sunshine? It is the way we can use our words, whether a verbal conversation, an email, or even a text, to shine that brightness and warmth into the lives of others.

> *"The hearts of the wise make their mouths prudent, and their lips promote instruction. Gracious words are a honeycomb, sweet to the soul and healing to the bones."*
> ~ Proverbs 16:23-24

Wise people have hearts that are right with God, which leads to them speaking wisely too. They think before they speak, knowing that our words can build others up or tear them down. It is much better to use our words to edify others in order to keep building the kingdom of God. Words that build others up are sweet as honey to taste both to those offering the words and those receiving them. This sweetness reaches the depths of our soul and brings healing to our body, mind, and spirit.

What are some benefits of verbal sunshine?

> *"Do not let any unwholesome talk come out of your mouths, but only what is helpful for building others up according to their needs, that it may benefit those who listen."*
> ~ Ephesians 4:29

It builds others up providing what they need when they need it. When we spread verbal sunshine, it warms the heart of the listener and enriches their life. Isn't it usually easier to tear others down or find fault with something they are doing? If we try to think before we speak and communicate more verbal sunshine, our hearts will be warmed and enriched even more. Verbal sunshine is free to shine into the lives of all we encounter.

What are some concrete ways to share verbal sunshine with someone?

> Share a sincere compliment about their character.
> Tell them how they have impacted your spiritual journey.
> Listen with your heart and ears.
> Let people know when you are praying for them.
> Tell someone you believe in them.
> Share the goodness that you see in them.

Be encouraged to…

> be generous with encouraging others.
> share little pieces of your heart full of love.
> seek ways to spread verbal sunshine everywhere you go.

REFLECTION:

What kind of verbal sunshine have you received recently?
Who is someone you can bless with verbal sunshine this week?

> *"I thank my God every time I remember you. In all my prayers for all of you, I always pray with joy because of your partnership in the gospel from the first day until now, being confident of this, that he who began a good work in you will carry it on to completion until the day of Christ Jesus. It is right for me to feel this way about all of you, since I have you in my heart and, whether I am in chains or defending and confirming the gospel, all of you share in God's grace with me."*
> ~ Philippians 1:3-7

15

The Twelve Days of Christmas

The Twelve Days of Christmas is a festive Christian season that starts with the celebration of Jesus' birth on December 25 and runs for twelve days. The twelfth day celebrates the Epiphany, which is when the Magi visited baby Jesus, bringing the gifts of gold, frankincense, and myrrh. The twelve days were a time of rededication and renewal. Children received small, simple, and usually symbolic gifts of faith.

What are the hidden Christian symbols found in The Twelve Days of Christmas that we can reflect on?

1ST Day: A PARTRIDGE IN A PEAR TREE

On Christmas Day, the first and greatest gift that is given to us is Jesus, the Son of God, the Word made flesh, the Light of the world; the divine coming in human form to dwell with us. The pear tree is symbolic of the wood of the tree—the cross that Jesus would eventually be hung on at His death. How appropriate that this gift is first because Jesus is the best gift ever given to this world—to you and me—that assures us of spending eternity with Him.

2ND Day: TWO TURTLE DOVES

The two turtle doves represent the Old and New Testaments of the Bible—the Word of God. With this gift, we have the whole story of the Christian faith and God's plan of salvation for the entire world at our fingertips. The Bible is a roadmap for our lives as we stand on His promises day by day.

3ᴿᴰ Day: Three French hens

The three French hens have a two-fold representation. One is the Trinity, which is the Father (God), the Son (Jesus), and the Holy Spirit. What a comfort to always have the Trinity accompanying us. The three French hens also represent the three theological virtues of faith, hope, and love.

"And now these three remain: faith, hope and love. But the greatest of these is love."
~ 1 Corinthians 13:13

We are given the virtues of faith, hope, and love that we can share with all. The greatest is love because

"...God is love."
~ 1 John 4:16

4ᵀᴴ Day: Four calling birds

These birds represent the four gospels of the New Testament, which call us to deeper intimacy with Jesus as they share accounts of His life. The stories are a beautiful song to our hearts as we grow in faith.

1-Matthew
2-Mark
3-Luke
4-John

5ᵀᴴ Day: Five gold rings

The five gold rings are indicative of the Torah of the Jewish people, which are the first five books of the Old Testament in the Christian Bible.

1-Genesis
2-Exodus
3-Leviticus

4-Numbers

5-Deuteronomy

6ᵀᴴ Day: Six geese a-laying

What a great correlation to the first story of the Bible, the Creation account. God formed the world and everything in it, in a sense "hatching" an egg a day for six days.

1-God created the heavens and the earth.

2-God created the sky and seas.

3-God created the land and plants.

4-God created the sun, moon, and the stars.

5-God created the fish and birds.

6-God created the animals and man.

7ᵀᴴ Day: Seven swans a-swimming

The seven swans, one of the most beautiful and graceful creatures on earth, represent the seven gifts of the Holy Spirit. They are spiritual gifts that help us grow in holiness, experience God's presence, and edify the Body of Christ.

"We have different gifts, according to the grace given to each of us. If your gift is prophesying, then prophesy in accordance with your faith; if it is serving, then serve; if it is teaching, then teach; if it is to encourage, then give encouragement; if it is giving, then give generously; if it is to lead, do it diligently; if it is to show mercy, do it cheerfully."
~ Romans 12:6-8

1-Prophecy

2-Serving

3-Teaching

4-Encouraging

5-Giving

6-Leading

7-Extending mercy

8ᵀᴴ Day: Eight maids-a-milking

Jesus came to save everyone—from the servant to royalty. In the song, these milkmaids represent those who receive His Word and grace and the eight Beatitudes.

"Blessed are…

1-the poor in spirit, for theirs is the kingdom of heaven.

2-those who mourn, for they shall be comforted.

3-the meek, for they shall inherit the earth.

4-those who hunger and thirst for righteousness, for they shall be filled.

5-the merciful, for they shall obtain mercy.

6-the pure in heart, for they shall see God.

7-the peacemakers, for they shall be called children of God.

8-they which are persecuted for righteousness sake, for theirs is the kingdom of heaven."

~ Matthew 5:3-10 (ESV)

9ᵀᴴ Day: Nine ladies dancing

The nine ladies dancing symbolize the gifts known as the fruit of the Spirit. The fruit of the Spirit are observable behaviors in people that flow from the Holy Spirit's presence in them.

"But the Holy Spirit produces this kind of fruit in our lives:

1-Love

2-Joy

3-Peace

4-Patience

5-Kindness

6-Goodness

7-Faithfulness

8-Gentleness

9-Self-control"

~ Galatians 5:22-23 (NLT)

10TH DAY: TEN LORDS A-LEAPING

How perfect to see the ten lords a-leaping, who were judges and in charge of the law, represent the Ten Commandments.

1-"Thou shall have no other gods before me.

2-Thou shalt not make unto thee any graven image.

3-Thou shalt not take the name of the Lord thy God in vain.

4-Remember the Sabbath Day to keep it holy.

5-Honor thy father and mother.

6-Thou shalt not kill.

7-Thou shalt not commit adultery.

8-Thou shalt not steal.

9-Thou shalt not bear false witness against thy neighbor.

10-Thou shalt not covet your neighbor's house, wife, servant, animals or anything."

~ Exodus 20:2-17

11TH DAY: ELEVEN PIPERS PIPING

The eleven faithful disciples who followed Jesus through until the end symbolize the eleven pipers piping. Judas Iscariot, the twelfth original disciple, betrayed Jesus and felt so bad that he committed suicide. The eleven continued to carry the gospel message.

1-Simon (whom He named Peter)

2-Andrew

3-James, son of Zebedee

4-John

5-Philip

6-Bartholomew

7-Thomas

8-Matthew, the tax collector

9-James, son of Alphaeus

10-Thaddeus

11-Simon, the Zealot

12ᵀᴴ Day: Twelve drummers drumming

The final gift of the twelve drummers drumming represents the twelve points of doctrine in the Apostles' Creed.

1-I believe in God, the Father almighty, creator of heaven and earth.

2-I believe in Jesus Christ His only Son, our Lord.

3-He was conceived by the power of the Holy Spirit and born of the Virgin Mary.

4-He suffered under Pontius Pilate, was crucified, died, and was buried.

5-He descended into hell. On the third day, He rose again.

6-He ascended into heaven and is seated at the right hand of God the Father almighty.

7-He will come again to judge the living and the dead.

8-I believe in the Holy Spirit,

9-the holy catholic Church, the communion of saints,

10-the forgiveness of sins,

11-the resurrection of the body,

12-and life everlasting.

In "The Twelve Days of Christmas" song, the gift from the first day, Jesus, is given all twelve days. Indeed, Jesus is the gift that keeps on giving!

Noticing that the gifts are cumulative, can you guess how many gifts are given throughout the twelve days? Feel free to figure it out and check my math; I'll post the answer at the end. *

Be encouraged to…

> thank God for the greatest gift of all time—Jesus!
> reflect on the beauty of all of God's creations.
> work on sharing one fruit of the Spirit that challenges you to grow.

REFLECTION:

Have you reflected on and thanked God for a spiritual gift that you possess?
Which Beatitude is most meaningful to you?

> *There are a total of 364 gifts—enough to last until next Christmas!

"May the Lord be with your spirit. And may his grace be with all of you."
~ 2 Timothy 4:22 (NLT)

16

Autumn Leaves

Autumn in upstate New York holds the most beautiful array of colorful leaves displaying God's glory at its finest. They are often breath-taking, especially with the many yellow and reds.

I thought about the life cycle of the leaves throughout the four seasons and some parallels with our lives and our faith.

When we first come to know about Jesus and start a personal relationship with Him, our faith is like the budding trees in the springtime. We are like newborns in our faith journey, slowly emerging like the new buds.

As time goes on and we grow deeper in faith, we start to flourish. We become like the summer trees full of lush green leaves as we stand tall and steadfast with Jesus.

Over time, our lives produce more beauty for the Lord, and our sense of community expands. As we participate in more ministries and share the love of Christ with others, we become even more beautifully colored, just like the autumn leaves. We blossom in our own way to form a piece of the Body of Christ.

Watching the autumn leaves fall from the trees symbolizes our life of service to others. We die more to ourselves, like the leaves that fall to the ground, so that Jesus may shine forth as we serve in love.

Christine M. Fisher

"And Jesus answered them, 'The hour has come for the Son of Man to be glorified. Truly, truly, I say to you, unless a grain of wheat falls into the earth and dies, it remains alone; but if it dies, it bears much fruit.'"
~ John 12:23-24 (ESV)

Jesus knew His ultimate purpose on earth was about to be fulfilled. He was to die on a cross so we would be free of our sin. The sacrifice of Jesus' life glorified God the Father. The death of Jesus, like when a grain of wheat falls to the earth, yields the greatest fruit for all who come to believe in Him.

After the leaves return to the earth, we know that winter will be coming. It is a time where everything looks barren, but beneath the snow and ice, we know life is still at work, which we witness when it turns to spring. The same is true in us; when we serve one another, new life is alive in us. We, too, experience the different seasons in our lives just like the leaves.

Be encouraged to…

> praise God for the beauty of the seasons.
> see how you might be of service to others.
> show gratitude to Jesus for laying down His life for you.
> reflect on what season the leaves are currently in your life.

REFLECTION:

What can you do to glorify the Son of Man today?
Who needs some of your fruit in their life?

"For the grace of God has appeared that offers salvation to all people. It teaches us to say 'No' to ungodliness and worldly passions, and to live self-controlled, upright and godly lives in this present age."
~ Titus 2:11-12

17

Exalt His Name

One of the main reasons I started writing was to share how God is at work in the ordinary of our lives. I marvel at the way God orchestrates our footsteps. Even though I often think I am in control, God gently reminds me how only He has the capacity to work everything out for our good.

"I will praise the Lord at all times. I will constantly speak his praises. I will boast only in the Lord; let all who are helpless take heart. Come, let us tell of the Lord's greatness; let us exalt his name together."
~ Psalm 34:1-3 (NLT)

We should constantly praise the Lord with our lips and in our hearts as we live with an attitude of gratitude. We can only boast about the Lord's goodness and power that flows through us; nothing that we do. Together, we can keep each other uplifted as we exchange stories of His greatness in our lives and exalt the name of the Lord.

In a matter of a few hours, I saw several little orchestrations that made me exalt the name of the Lord. My day started with going to a church event, followed by an annual check-up, and then meeting a friend, who was picking me up from my appointment.

I grabbed a bag from my car to store some items I was bringing in. I laughed at God as I marveled and wondered how He made a dirt heart appear randomly on the bag.

The medical assistant was a delight—very kind, genuine, and caring. At the end, I said to her, *"You don't have to answer this, but I have a strange* question. *Are you a Christian?"* She said, *"Yes, I am, and that's not a strange question."* I felt inspired to give her my latest book, *God's Glory Manifested.* We chatted for a few minutes, and I was surprised to hear she does some writing too. It was a lovely encounter that God orchestrated with the sequences of events.

As I was waiting for my friend to pick me up, I saw a co-worker drive by and wave. She has been experiencing some health issues for the last few months. I did not get to check in with her before I left work the day before, and I was wondering how she was. Something inspired me to think maybe she was going to the pharmacy next door, so I walked that way. Sure enough, her car was there, and I was able to get an update.

What I realized about the orchestrations that I shared is that they were dependent on the "little" detail of who God provided for me to meet with. I originally had other plans that did not work out because this particular friend was the one I was supposed to meet with. Because of meeting her where I did, I had a book with me to give to the medical assistant, with an extra one to give to my friend, and also to see my co-worker. God filled my heart with joy to see the events unfold for His glory.

I remain in awe at seeing the little details in our lives where God is working. We have the privilege of praising the Lord continually and sharing His greatness with one another. Together we exalt His name.

Be encouraged to…

> praise the Lord at all times.
> share with others how you see the Lord working in your life.
> tell of the Lord's goodness.
> exalt the name of the Lord.
> be in awe of God's orchestrations.
> know God is always working for your good.

REFLECTION:

What was the latest God-orchestrated moment you experienced?
Who are you inspired to share an "only God" moment with?

> *"All this is for your benefit, so that the grace that is reaching more and more people may cause thanksgiving to overflow to the glory of God."*
> ~ 2 Corinthians 4:15

18

Celebrating #500

My heart overflows with joy as I celebrate God's faithfulness and goodness with this being the 500th reflection for hopetoinspireyou.com! He has provided me with weekly inspiration about His working in the ordinary of life throughout the last ten years plus.

To capture joy,

we must cast

a net of gratitude.

"You make known to me the path of life; in your presence there is fullness of joy; at your right hand are pleasures forevermore."
~ Psalm 16:11 (ESV)

This verse equates joy with God's presence. He shows us the path our lives should go as He leads and guides us when our hearts are open to Him. His mighty right hand is always there to shower us with His goodness.

I can testify to this truth with my writing ministry. I experience joy, which I feel is God's presence as I see how He reveals Himself in the ordinary of life and share that through writing. Joy and peace fill my heart when another reflection gets to the "right" stage to publish.

"Don't be drunk with wine, because that will ruin your life. Instead, be filled with the Holy Spirit, singing psalms and hymns and spiritual songs among yourselves, and making music

to the Lord in your hearts. And give thanks for everything to
God the Father in the name of our Lord Jesus Christ."
~ Ephesians 5:18-20 (NLT)

We are encouraged to be thankful for and in everything, as we have the most important gift in life—God, Jesus, and the Holy Spirit to accompany us. The presence of the Spirit in us makes praise flow from our mouths and hearts as we have gratitude for all that God provides and orchestrates.

Have you ever viewed gratitude as a way of praising and showing God honor for His goodness and grace that you experience? This writing ministry has helped me to be accountable to see and have gratitude for life's small wonders and blessings. I grow in awe of our Creator when I think about all the little intricacies that He orchestrates. Gratitude can be a deliberate act of opening our hearts to the beauty and goodness that is all around us because God made everything good.

"Shout with joy to the Lord, all the earth! For the Lord
is good. His unfailing love continues forever, and his
faithfulness continues to each generation."
~ Psalm 100:1, 5 (NLT)

We are encouraged to shout with joy to the Lord for His goodness and faithfulness. Our great God is continually lavishing us with His love and faithfulness—to all generations!

My website started as a "test" to see if God would provide weekly inspiration after seeing other online bloggers. I am forever grateful for the series of events and people that God put in my path, which led to that first post on September 5, 2014. When I wrote that first post, I had no idea what God had in store for me! I faithfully continued writing through the years because He keeps the inspiration coming.

Christine M. Fisher

About five years in, readers suggested I put some reflections in book form. God orchestrated events that led me to meet a self-published author from Texas, and a year and a half later, she was the publisher of my first book, *God's Presence Illuminated*.

Little did I know that writing would become my unconventional "ministry"—the way He gave me to share Christ and faith with others. He gives me the courage to share a book with a stranger, and this often leads to discussing faith and even to a new spiritual brother or sister in the Lord to journey with. My world was small before this ministry, but God has opened my eyes and heart to have personally shared about 1,900 of my books with others. He is a good, good God who is faithful. God has enabled me to do what I'm doing because of His grace.

The two greatest gifts of this writing ministry are the growth in me personally as well as spiritually and meeting people who inspire my faith walk. It is refreshing to grow deeper and deeper in intimacy with the Lord and in my faith. Thank you for being a part of this ministry—for gracing me with your presence in my life.

What are some of the things in my net of gratitude that have brought me joy with this ministry?

> Learning to embrace and celebrate who and how God made me.
> Being able to meet and learn so many spirit-filled people's stories.
> Growing in trust, seeing God provide little nuggets of inspiration to share.
> Publishing four books to date, so more lives can be reached.
> Stretching myself as speaking engagements come along.
> Gracing me with spiritual family to journey with.
> Becoming more confident knowing God is working in and through me.
> God providing the path with this ministry.

The provision of the titles of the books and living them out.
Seeing God's timing each step of this journey.
Using my God-given gifts to fulfill His purpose for my life.
The editors, publisher, encouragers, and faithful readers who journey with me.

Be encouraged to…

seek His presence in the little details so your joy may be full.
practice gratitude in all circumstances—the good and bad.
pay attention to seeing God's goodness and faithfulness.
use your gifts to glorify Him while enjoying the adventure.
know God provides everything in His perfect timing.

REFLECTION:

What brings you joy in your spiritual journey?
What surprise has God provided in one of your ministries?

"Each time he said, 'My grace is all you need. My power works best in weakness.' So now I am glad to boast about my weaknesses, so that the power of Christ can work through me."
~ 2 Corinthians 12:9 (NLT)

19

Let Us Begin

"Yesterday is gone.
Tomorrow has not yet come.
We have only today.
Let us begin."
~ Mother Teresa

YESTERDAY IS GONE.

The past is gone. We cannot change what has happened in the past or live in the past. However, it is beneficial to remember what God has done in our lives.

"Remember the wonders he has done, his miracles,
and the judgments he pronounced."
~ Psalm 105:5

Remembering how God has worked in our lives through His various orchestrations gives us hope that He will continue to care for us today, in the present.

TOMORROW HAS NOT YET COME.

Life is finite. We cannot live for tomorrow because we never know how many tomorrows we have. When we realize this truth, it helps us to avoid procrastinating and to work on the important things that matter in the present.

"Why, you do not even know what will happen tomorrow. What is your life? You are a mist that appears for a little while and then vanishes."
~ James 4:14

Though we like to make plans for our tomorrows, it is important to remember that we only have tomorrow if God wills it for us.

WE HAVE ONLY TODAY.

Concentrate on today. We can seize today, which is ready to be filled with new opportunities and graces. We get to choose how we respond to today, living as if this may be our last day.

"This is the day that the Lord has made; let us rejoice and be glad in it."
~ Psalm 118:24 (ESV)

Rejoice in the gift of today that God gives us. Yes, rejoice and be glad in the present.

LET US BEGIN.

Can you think of a small change you want to make regarding something physical, spiritual, emotional, or intellectual that you want to improve upon?

Do you want to…

> be inspired to show an act of kindness to one person daily?
> make time to take a ten minute walk around the block?
> focus on one attribute you can emulate to be more Christ-like?
> take care of paperwork right away?
> change one thing to improve your physical health?
> have a more positive attitude when things start going wrong?
> take a few minutes to study something that interests you?
> say no to that extra cup of coffee?

Can I challenge you each day to take at least ONE step forward to change for the better?

When I intentionally take one step to become a better me, it helps me know I can do more, little by little. It encourages me to keep finding ways to grow.

Be encouraged knowing…

> yesterday is history.
> tomorrow might not come.
> today is the day of opportunities and graces.
> today is the day to begin anew.
> you can't change yesterday.
> you can't control tomorrow.
> you can make the most of today.
> every day counts.

Go live life to the fullest today!

REFLECTION:

Which part of the quote do you need to work on most?
What is one change you can focus on to make the most of today?

"Grace and peace to you from God our Father and the Lord Jesus Christ. Praise be to the God and Father of our Lord Jesus Christ, who has blessed us in the heavenly realms with every spiritual blessing in Christ."
- Ephesians 1:2-3

20

Joyful Appreciation

"Giving thanks warms the soul and reminds us that
life is an extraordinary privilege. Joy doesn't come from
having, but from appreciating what we have."
~ Matthew Kelly

When we live from a place of giving thanks and gratitude, doesn't it warm our soul? It helps to keep in mind that all we are and have is a gift from God, who is worthy of our thanks and gratitude continually.

"Rejoice always, pray without ceasing, give thanks in all
circumstances; for this is the will of God in Christ Jesus for you."
~ 1 Thessalonians 5:16-18 (ESV)

Isn't it easy to rejoice, pray, and be thankful when things are going good, but a challenge when we suffer and endure trials? When Paul wrote this letter to the Thessalonian church, they were facing great persecution and internal disputes having many reasons not to be joyful. Paul reminds them, along with us, that no matter our circumstances, we need to rejoice and be thankful because we know joy comes from our dependence on God.

What can we give thanks for to warm our soul?

Waking up to a new day.

Trials that bring us closer to Jesus in His suffering for our salvation.

Being able to worship without fear of persecution.

Every day is an extraordinary privilege. This life allows us to be Christ-bearers as we share His love, presence, and compassion with others. When we rise each day, we are filled with hope for what the Lord has in store for the day. His mercies are new every morning.

> *"For you have been given not only the privilege of trusting*
> *in Christ but also the privilege of suffering for him."*
> ~ Philippians 1:29 (NLT)

Isn't it a great privilege to live day by day knowing we can trust Christ? Have you considered that it is also a privilege to suffer too? Christ's death on the cross was intense suffering that He willingly endured so we can have eternal life. How much more should we count it a privilege to know the crosses we bear help us enter into oneness with Christ? We have assurance that Christ is with us in our suffering.

What are examples of life's extraordinary privileges?

> Loving others with God's great agape love.
> Praying with someone in need.
> Enduring hardship to enter into Jesus' suffering.

JOY COMES FROM APPRECIATING WHAT WE HAVE RATHER THAN HAVING.

Our material possessions might bring us happiness, but they do not bring us joy. It is about appreciating what we have in the Spirit rather than having the temporary things of this world like a mansion or an expensive car.

> *"For the kingdom of God is not a matter of eating and drinking*
> *but of righteousness and peace and joy in the Holy Spirit.*
> *Whoever thus serves Christ is acceptable to God and approved by men."*
> ~ Romans 14:17-18 (ESV)

The kingdom of God is not about physical materials. Joy is a fruit of the Spirit that we receive from knowing God, abiding with Christ, and being filled with the Holy Spirit. The Holy Spirit's gifts of love, peace, goodness, and righteous are what bring us joy. Joy is an attitude requiring an action, not an emotion.

What things do we have that we can appreciate to fill us with joy?

Spiritual friendships.
> The "God moments" we experience.
>> The ability to worship and commune with God daily.

Be encouraged to…

> rejoice even in difficult circumstances.
> have an attitude of prayer continually.
> practice giving thanks in all circumstances.
> reflect on the extraordinary privilege of trusting Christ.
> know even our suffering is a privilege because we join in Christ's suffering.
> be filled with joy that is the fruit of appreciation.

"Find the gratitude in your life, and you'll find joy standing right next to it."
~ Melody Beattie

REFLECTION:

What suffering have you endured and been able to see God at work in? What is something small you have great appreciation for?

> *"Grace, mercy, and peace, which come from God the Father and from Jesus Christ—the Son of the Father—will continue to be with us who live in truth and love."*
> ~ 2 John 1:3 (NLT)

21

Stand Tall

I enjoy gazing upon God's masterpiece creations of trees, plants, flowers and hills. Seeing three different scenarios of huge trees made me think of parallels with our lives.

THEY HAVE STRONG FOUNDATIONS AS THEIR BASE.

> *"So now you Gentiles are no longer strangers and foreigners. You are citizens along with all of God's holy people. You are members of God's family. Together, we are his house, built on the foundation of the apostles and the prophets. And the cornerstone is Christ Jesus himself. We are carefully joined together in him, becoming a holy temple for the Lord."*
> ~ Ephesians 2:19-21 (NLT)

The foundation of our faith is based first on the cornerstone of Christ Jesus Himself. The building of faith continued when Jesus appointed apostles and prophets to proclaim the good news of salvation. As descendants of them, you and I are members of God's family being linked to Jesus, the cornerstone. Our bodies become holy temples of the Lord.

BEAUTY GROWS FROM STRONG FOUNDATIONS.

> *"And now, just as you accepted Christ Jesus as your Lord, you must continue to follow him. Let your roots grow down into him, and let your lives be built on him. Then your faith will grow strong in the truth you were taught, and you will overflow with thankfulness."*
> ~ Colossians 2:6-7 (NLT)

As we stay rooted deeply in Jesus, who is our strong foundation, our lives grow more and more in producing His beauty. We recall the truth Jesus shared in word and deed to help our faith grow stronger. It creates more beauty as we are filled with gratitude for all Jesus does for us that we can share with those we encounter.

FROM THE CENTER COME THE TALL BRANCHES, WHICH STAND STRONG AMONG ALL THE BEAUTY.

> *"Be on your guard; stand firm in the faith; be*
> *courageous; be strong. Do everything in love."*
> ~ 1 Corinthians 16:13-14

We can stand proud and firm in our faith, living courageously and strong in the Lord. Often, we may feel different from the world because of our resolve to do everything in love, trying to share the love we experience from God. We get to be beacons of light standing tall as we share the bounty of goodness we have been shown.

The Scripture below is my prayer and encouragement for you. May you stand tall being the majestic cedar that God made.

> *"'This is what the Sovereign Lord says: I will take a branch from the*
> *top of a tall cedar, and I will plant it on the top of Israel's highest*
> *mountain. It will become a majestic cedar, sending forth its branches*
> *and producing seed. Birds of every sort will nest in it, finding shelter*
> *in the shade of its branches. And all the trees will know that it is I,*
> *the Lord, who cuts the tall tree down and makes the short tree grow*
> *tall. It is I who makes the green tree wither and gives the dead tree*
> *new life. I, the Lord, have spoken, and I will do what I said!'"*
> ~ Ezekiel 17:22-24 (NLT)

Christine M. Fisher

Be encouraged to…

stay deeply rooted in the foundation of Christ Jesus.
rejoice in the beauty of growth in you because of Jesus.
stand tall and firm in your faith, sharing His love.

REFLECTION:

What is one way you can deepen your foundation in Christ?
How can you stand more firmly in your faith?

*"Yet the Lord longs to be gracious to you; therefore he
will rise up to show you compassion. For the Lord is a
God of justice. Blessed are all who wait for him!"*
~ Isaiah 30:18

22

Changing the Present

"NO amount of
REGRET
changes the past.

NO amount of
ANXIETY
changes the future.

ANY amount of
GRATITUDE
changes the present."
~ Ann Voskamp

NO AMOUNT OF REGRET CHANGES THE PAST.

When we think about regrets, it is safe to say that we all have our fair share of them because they are part of life. Regrets are either the result of us realizing we did something sinful, maybe unintentionally, or thinking that we made wrong choices with decisions we have made. The most important thing is to not get stuck dwelling on our regrets because they do not have the power to change the past. What if we looked at our regrets with grace, knowing we did the best we could at the time with the knowledge we had?

Have you considered that even God had regrets?

"The Lord saw how great the wickedness of the human race had become on the earth, and that every inclination of the thoughts of

Christine M. Fisher

the human heart was only evil all the time. The Lord regretted that
he had made human beings on the earth, and his heart was deeply
troubled. So the Lord said, 'I will wipe from the face of the earth the
human race I have created—and with them the animals, the birds
and the creatures that move along the ground—for I regret that I
have made them.' But Noah found favor in the eyes of the Lord."
~ Genesis 6:5-8

In Hebrew, the word "regret" translates to "sigh." We know God does not make mistakes, so we can interpret this passage as God feeling sorrow for the direction this world was going. Since God is omniscient, He knew sin would have consequences. Sin grieves His heart, as He wants to have constant fellowship with us, His beloved. God had Noah and his family build an ark to keep them and all of creation that God instructed them to bring on the ark, thus saving the human race.

"If we confess our sins, he is faithful and just and
will forgive us our sins and purify us from all unrighteousness."
~ 1 John 1:9

If our regrets are caused by sin, we should confess them and repent so we can live in freedom from the past. God forgives and forgets; so should we.

"And we know that in all things God works for the good
of those who love him, who have been called according to his purpose."
~ Romans 8:28

One thing to remember about regret is that God is still God, and He can make good out of our choices.

NO AMOUNT OF ANXIETY CHANGES THE FUTURE.

In our humanity, it is natural to have some anxiety. We never know what the future holds, and we know there are several variables that factor in. When we know we can't control things, we have more anxiety. But no matter how much anxiety we incur, it does nothing to change the future. What if, when we start to feel that anxiety build up, we say, *"Jesus, I trust in you. I know you love me, care for me, and provide everything I need."*

> *"Look at the birds of the air: they neither sow nor reap nor gather into barns, and yet your heavenly Father feeds them. Are you not of more value than they? And which of you by being anxious can add a single hour to his span of life?"*
> ~ Matthew 6:26-27 (ESV)

Jesus assures us that we, as humans, are even more valuable than the birds of the air that He looks after. Birds don't have minds like we do, so they don't have worries or anxieties and cannot plan ahead. God provides food for the birds as they live moment by moment. Jesus reminds us that anxiety does not help us accomplish anything, and He values us even more than the birds.

> *"For your kingdom is an everlasting kingdom. You rule throughout all generations. The Lord always keeps his promises; he is gracious in all he does."*
> ~ Psalm 145:13 (NLT)

A great antidote to anxiety is to abide with Christ and stand on His promises that we find in Scripture. He is a promise keeper, and we can always depend on Him.

ANY AMOUNT OF GRATITUDE CHANGES THE PRESENT.

Especially when we are going through difficult times, any amount of gratitude we can muster can help change our attitude in the present. What a gift it is to celebrate the present with hearts full of gratitude for even the smallest of blessings that God graces us with. The more we are able to be grateful, the more we see God's goodness in our world.

> *"The crowd joined in the attack against Paul and Silas, and the magistrates ordered them to be stripped and beaten with rods. After they had been severely flogged, they were thrown into prison, and the jailer was commanded to guard them carefully. When he received these orders, he put them in the inner cell and fastened their feet in the stocks. About midnight Paul and Silas were praying and singing hymns to God, and the other prisoners were listening to them. Suddenly there was such a violent earthquake that the foundations of the prison were shaken. At once all the prison doors flew open, and everyone's chains came loose."*
> ~ Acts 16:22-26

Imagine being Paul or Silas, who were just stripped, flogged with rods, thrown into prison, and their feet put in stocks. Despite their desperate circumstances, they were present in the moment and decided to give glory and praise, a form of gratitude, to God by praying and singing hymns to Him. That led to the jailer and his whole family being saved when he took Paul and Silas to his house to tend to their wounds that night. Even more amazing to me is that Paul and Silas returned to jail by morning so that the jailer would not get in trouble. What a beautiful testament to how gratitude in all circumstances changes the present.

Be encouraged to reflect on how...

no amount of regret changes the past, but God can use it for good.
no amount of anxiety changes the future, but Jesus keeps His promises.
cultivating a spirit of gratitude betters your present.

REFLECTION:

When was a time you saw God make good out of a regret you had?
When did you exercise a spirit of gratitude despite difficult circumstances?

"Rejoice always, pray without ceasing, give thanks in all circumstances; for this is the will of God in Christ Jesus for you. The grace of our Lord Jesus Christ be with you."
~ 1 Thessalonians 5:16-17, 28 (ESV)

23

Christmas To-Do List

It might not be the Christmas season when you are reading this, but it technically applies every day.

Rather than just BUY PRESENTS—BE PRESENT!

"Jesus replied, 'No one who puts a hand to the plow and looks back is fit for service in the kingdom of God.'"
~ Luke 9:62

"Therefore do not be anxious about tomorrow, for tomorrow will be anxious for itself. Sufficient for the day is its own trouble."
~ Matthew 6:34 (ESV)

Jesus encourages us to not focus on the past or the future. It is most important to be present in the present moment, which is a gift to enjoy and make the best of. We should give our total attention to the people we are with and share God's love and concern. Be present today and live life to the fullest. Tomorrow is never promised.

Do you need to consciously work on living in the present moment?

Rather than just WRAP GIFTS—WRAP SOMEONE IN A HUG!

"People were bringing little children to Jesus for him to place his hands on them, but the disciples rebuked them. When Jesus saw this, he was indignant. He said to them, 'Let the little children come to me, and do not hinder them, for the kingdom of God belongs to such as these. Truly I tell you, anyone who will not receive the kingdom of God like a little child will never enter it.' And he took the children in his arms, placed his hands on them and blessed them."
~ Mark 10:13-16

Jesus gave us an example of how everyone, even the little child, is important to Him. He pointed out how we need to be childlike in our faith, trusting and embracing Jesus in love. Embracing others can impart divine love and care, which is a beautiful way to share Jesus with others. Jesus not only embraced the little children, but He blessed them too.

Have you blessed people while embracing them with Jesus' love?

Rather than just SEND GIFTS—SEND PEACE!

"Peace I leave with you; my peace I give you. I do not give to you as the world gives. Do not let your hearts be troubled and do not be afraid."
~ John 14:27

"Make every effort to keep the unity of the Spirit through the bond of peace."
~ Ephesians 4:3

Jesus lived in peace throughout His life—even when He was on the cross. Before Jesus died, He told His disciples He gave that same peace to them. Since we, too, are Jesus' disciples, we have that same access to His peace. The world itself does not understand that peace. We can live in faith, not fear, because of it. We, through the Spirit, extend that peace to all we encounter.

Are you able to share the peace of Jesus that is in you with others?

Rather than just SHOP FOR FOOD—DONATE FOOD!

"Everything in the world is about to be wrapped up, so take nothing for granted. Stay wide-awake in prayer. Most of all, love each other as if your life depended on it. Love makes up for practically anything. Be quick to give a meal to the hungry, a bed to the homeless—cheerfully."
~ 1 Peter 4:7-9 (MSG)

Scripture encourages us to truly love others with all that we have. When we do, we are following in Jesus' footsteps; He loved not just the righteous but even the worst of sinners. As we grow in love, we put our love into action. We desire to feed the hungry, shelter the homeless, and visit the infirmed.

What is one new way you can put your love into action?

Rather than just SEE THE LIGHTS—BE THE LIGHT!

"When Jesus spoke again to the people, he said, 'I am the light of the world. Whoever follows me will never walk in darkness, but will have the light of life.'"
~ John 8:12

"You are the light of the world. A town built on a hill cannot be hidden. Neither do people light a lamp and put it under a bowl. Instead they put it on its stand, and it gives light to everyone in the house. In the same way, let your light shine before others, that they may see your good deeds and glorify your Father in heaven."
~ Matthew 5:14-16

Jesus is the true light of the world. He entered the darkness of this world so that we can have the light. Jesus says we are the light of the world. Our lights will shine with the good we do and how we glorify God, our Father; our lights will shine and help guide others.

Do others see Jesus' light shine through you and your actions?

Be encouraged to…

consciously be present in the moments of life.
share Jesus' love through an embrace and blessing.
help someone experience Jesus' deep-seated peace.
feed someone in need.
illuminate the path for someone who is struggling to find the way.

REFLECTION:

Which one of the "To-Do List" items do you need to work on most? Who can you reach out to in order to bless their day?

"Listen, my son, to your father's instruction and do not forsake your mother's teaching. They are a garland to grace your head and a chain to adorn your neck."
~ Proverbs 1:8-9

24

Make the Days Count

I received another insightful nugget of wisdom from my inspiring friend, Greg. After spending time with someone you are trying to encourage, do you, too, feel more spiritually alive?

"Don't count the days. Make the days count."
~ Muhammad Ali

This quote had even more significance coming from Greg, as he has been in the hospital for three months with a feeding tube in his stomach and losing the limited mobility he had left in his legs.

Greg embodies and lives out the truth of this quote each day of his life, especially throughout the last 43 years of facing physical challenges. He has endured so much with physical limitations yet remains positive and steadfast in his faith, making each day count by figuring out ways he can bring the love and joy of God to others, as well as remaining close to God.

"Teach us to number our days, that we may gain a heart of wisdom."
~ Psalm 90:12

This is insight Moses wrote that fits perfectly with the quote Greg shared. Rather than counting the days until an event is supposed to happen or we get something done, we should focus on making the most of today, God's gift to us. None of us knows when God will call us home. Each day has endless opportunities for our hearts to grow in the love and wisdom of God.

The quote and Scripture bring us comfort and are good reminders to reflect on, especially on our birthdays. No matter who we are, young or old, or what our circumstances are, we should focus on making each day count.

What are some ways we can make each day count?

Be good stewards of what God has given us, both materially and spiritually.

"God blessed them and said to them, 'Be fruitful and increase in number; fill the earth and subdue it. Rule over the fish in the sea and the birds in the sky and over every living creature that moves on the ground.'"
~ Genesis 1:28

"And all the believers met together in one place and shared everything they had. They sold their property and possessions and shared the money with those in need. They worshiped together at the Temple each day, met in homes for the Lord's Supper, and shared their meals with great joy and generosity."
~ Acts 2:44-46 (NLT)

"Each of you should use whatever gift you have received to serve others, as faithful stewards of God's grace in its various forms."
~ 1 Peter 4:10

Being made in God's image, we have the responsibility of being stewards of all the creation that He fashioned. God also gave us material possessions and has blessed each of us with spiritual gifts. Are we good stewards of creation and our material possessions? Are we sharing our unique spiritual gifts and God's grace to build up the Body of Christ?

Live sensibly and with intentionality.

"Be very careful, then, how you live—not as unwise but as wise, making the most of every opportunity, because the days are evil. Therefore

Christine M. Fisher

do not be foolish, but understand what the Lord's will is. Do not get drunk on wine, which leads to debauchery. Instead, be filled with the Spirit, speaking to one another with psalms, hymns, and songs from the Spirit. Sing and make music from your heart to the Lord, always giving thanks to God the Father for everything, in the name of our Lord Jesus Christ. Submit to one another out of reverence for Christ."
~ Ephesians 5:15-21

As Christians, it is our responsibility to live wisely, sensibly, and with intentionality. God's word encourages us to be filled with the Spirit, to share with each other about God working in our lives, and to see how the Word of God comes alive to us. Our hearts should be overflowing with songs of thanksgiving and gratitude for everything we experience in this life. Because of Christ in us, we love and care for each other.

Seek to grow in God's wisdom.

"Anyone who listens to my teaching and follows it is wise, like a person who builds a house on solid rock."
~ Matthew 7:24 (NLT)

"Who is wise and understanding among you? Let them show it by their good life, by deeds done in the humility that comes from wisdom. But if you harbor bitter envy and selfish ambition in your hearts, do not boast about it or deny the truth. Such 'wisdom' does not come down from heaven but is earthly, unspiritual, demonic. For where you have envy and selfish ambition, there you find disorder and every evil practice. But the wisdom that comes from heaven is first of all pure; then peace-loving, considerate, submissive, full of mercy and good fruit, impartial and sincere. Peacemakers who sow in peace reap a harvest of righteousness."
~ James 3:13-18

Being able to seek and grow in God's wisdom is a gift that we, as humans, can be filled with. If we read Scripture, follow Jesus' teachings, pray, and take time to be still and listen to God, we gain more wisdom. When we see lives filled with virtuous deeds, humility, pureness, peace, sincerity, and mercy, among other fruits of the Spirit, we know God's wisdom is dwelling.

Be encouraged to...

> make each day count and live it to the fullest in God's kingdom.
> practice better stewardship with all God has entrusted to you personally in the world, both materially and spiritually.
> live more sensibly and with intentionality, blessing others.
> grow more in wisdom by spending more time with God.

REFLECTION:

What is one action item you can implement to live more sensibly?
How can you be a better steward of a spiritual gift God has graced you with?

> *"Likewise, you who are younger, be subject to the elders. Clothe yourselves, all of you, with humility toward one another, for 'God opposes the proud but gives grace to the humble.'"*
> ~ 1 Peter 5:5 (ESV)

25

Help Me See Clearly

There's a first time for everything, and sometimes we hope it's the only time, right? It was a small thing, but it provided food for thought. My traveling buddy and I were meeting up to drive to a Christian concert a few hours away. I gathered all my belongings on what was a sunny day. About halfway into the trip I said, *"Oh, no. I'm sure I forgot my regular glasses,"* as I was donning my sunglasses. Sure enough, I looked through my bag to no avail.

I was determined to make the best of it because, truth be told, I often take my glasses off, especially when needing to read something. At the concert, I was able to secure a seat in the third row near center stage. The screen with the lyrics on it was big enough for me to see; I just couldn't clearly see the faces or eyes of the people on stage.

When I was dropped off at my car, I was relieved to find my regular glasses.

It made me think about our walk with the Lord and our faith.

How often do we not see clearly in our faith journey?

Do we ask Jesus to help us see clearly like He does?

*"They came to Bethsaida, and some people brought a blind man
and begged Jesus to touch him. He took the blind man by the hand
and led him outside the village. When he had spit on the man's eyes
and put his hands on him, Jesus asked, 'Do you see anything?' He
looked up and said, 'I see people; they look like trees walking around.'
Once more Jesus put his hands on the man's eyes. Then his eyes were
opened, his sight was restored, and he saw everything clearly."*
~ Mark 8:22-25

The blind man in this story had "community" that brought him to Jesus, and they begged Him to touch the man. Notice how Jesus was more than willing to grasp the hand of the blind man to lead him away from the crowd. I never noticed that Jesus spit directly on the man's eyes and then placed His healing hands on the blind man's eyes. The blind man could not see clearly the first time, so Jesus' hands touched his eyes again, and then he could see everything clearly.

Sometimes healings or miracles come in stages—it isn't always an immediate response.

> Sometimes we experience growth over time and learn to be patient. It is important to remember that God is always working, even if we don't see it.

> > With this story, I can't help but wonder if the trees that the man first saw representing people were a recognition that Jesus would die on the tree of life, the cross, for our salvation.

If we view our lives as trees, what is our response to these questions?

> How deep do your roots go?

> > How plentiful are your leaves or the fruit that grows from your life?

Be encouraged to…

> > reach out to those in your "community" that need Jesus' healing touch.
> > feel Jesus' hand grasping yours as He leads.
> > ask Jesus what healing needs to take place in you.
> > pray to see clearly like Jesus does.

REFLECTION:

What healing is needed in your life that Jesus is bringing to mind?
Can you recount a time when you witnessed a two-step healing?

> Jesus, please help us keep our eyes always clearly fixed on you.
> Please help adjust our vision when things are unclear, when they
> are out of focus, or when we lose our focus. Gently guide us to see
> with the eyes of our hearts and our eyes clearly as we trust you.
> We pray in Jesus' precious name. Amen.

> *"So prepare your minds for action and exercise self-control.*
> *Put all your hope in the gracious salvation that will come*
> *to you when Jesus Christ is revealed to the world."*
> ~ 1 Peter 1:13 (NLT)

26

Holy Moments

I often experience "God moments." These are things that can't just happen by chance but rather are the result of a greater power. God is at work.

God reveals His glory and goodness in our simple, ordinary lives. He is not just for the elite or those in high power. He loves us dearly and wants us to notice Him.

I heard two sermons that inspired this reflection. The pastor called the events, as I described them, "holy moments." The definition of "holy" from the Oxford Languages Online Dictionary is: "dedicated or consecrated to God or a religious purpose; sacred." "Holy," according to thenivbible.com, defines it as: "being separate or set apart."

Have you considered…

> that the word holy does not mean being perfect?
> your life as sacred and dedicated to God?
> that you personally are set apart as God's chosen one?
> that the ordinary moments in our lives can be "holy moments?"

Isn't it accurate to say that a "holy moment" is one where the following three characteristics are present?

GOD IS PRESENT.

> *"'Am I a God who is only close at hand?' says the Lord.*
> *'No, I am far away at the same time. Can anyone*
> *hide from me in a secret place?*

Am I not everywhere in all the heavens and earth?' says the Lord."
~ Jeremiah 23:23-24 (NLT)

The Lord reminds us that we can never hide from Him because He is truly everywhere in both heaven and earth. There is no place that God's power and knowledge does not extend to. God is the only One who is omnipresent, able to be present everywhere.

GOD IS ACTIVELY AT WORK.

> *"So, because Jesus was doing these things on the Sabbath, the Jewish leaders began to persecute him. In his defense Jesus said to them, 'My Father is always at his work to this very day, and I too am working.'"*
> ~ John 5:16-17

We learn that God, Jesus, and the Spirit are always at work on this earth. Isn't it comforting to know that as we go about our daily lives? How often do we think we are in control of our lives? It is freeing to live knowing that we are not in control. God is!

WE ARE TOTALLY PRESENT AND AWARE.

> *"As Jesus and his disciples were on their way, he came to a village where a woman named Martha opened her home to him. She had a sister called Mary, who sat at the Lord's feet listening to what he said. But Martha was distracted by all the preparations that had to be made. She came to him and asked, 'Lord, don't you care that my sister has left me to do the work by myself? Tell her to help me!' 'Martha, Martha,' the Lord answered, 'you are worried and upset about many things, but few things are needed—or indeed only one. Mary has chosen what is better, and it will not be taken away from her.'"*
> ~ Luke 10:38-42

How often are we distracted, like Martha? When we are distracted, we are not in the present moment. We take our eyes off of what is most important in life—our relationship with the Lord. Mary, taking time to just be in Jesus' presence and listening to Him, had her priorities in order. She was totally present, not being distracted, and aware of the most important thing in life.

One special "holy moment" I experienced was the result of God's orchestration of unusual circumstances. I adjusted my work schedule a bit this week and needed to drop something off for a friend at the church I grew up at. The church was open, so I took the opportunity to spend a few minutes with the Lord. It was a surprise to hear and see someone playing the pipe organ. I sat there, reminiscing about special encounters I experienced at the church while growing up. I was in awe of the beauty of the church, especially since it was renovated a few years ago. All of the décor is as I remembered it from my childhood. Listening to the music, so loud and powerful, brought tears to my eyes as I sat in God's presence. When the musician started playing "Amazing Grace," I couldn't help but think of how far I've come in my spiritual walk through the years. It was definitely a "holy moment" basking in God's grace as I took time to "just be" and savoring the beauty of the moment.

Be encouraged to…

> take time to reflect or journal on the word "holy."
> focus on experiencing God's presence with you continually.
> thank God for being at work in your life.
> practice being truly present in the moment.
> be more aware of "holy moments" and share one with someone.

BE BLESSED SEEING THE ORDINARY MOMENTS TURN INTO "HOLY MOMENTS!"

Christine M. Fisher

REFLECTION:

Which of the three characteristics do you need to work on in your life? What was the last "holy moment" you experienced as you took time to be present in the moment, not being distracted?

"For our boast is this, the testimony of our conscience, that we behaved in the world with simplicity and godly sincerity, not by earthly wisdom but by the grace of God, and supremely so toward you."
~ 2 Corinthians 1:12 (ESV)

27

Grateful

"To be grateful is to recognize the Love of God in everything He has given us—and He has given us everything. Every breath we draw is a gift of His love, every moment of existence is a grace, for it brings with it immense graces from Him. Gratitude therefore takes nothing for granted, is never unresponsive, is constantly awakening to new wonder and to praise of the goodness of God. For the grateful person knows that God is good, not by hearsay but by experience. And that is what makes all the difference."
~ Thomas Merton

Let's take a few moments to consider the true depth of the quote.

TO BE GRATEFUL IS TO RECOGNIZE THE LOVE OF GOD IN EVERYTHING HE HAS GIVEN US—AND HE HAS GIVEN US EVERYTHING.

Isn't it powerful to consider that being grateful can be linked to seeing God's love in everything He has given us in this life?

"By his divine power, God has given us everything we need for living a godly life. We have received all of this by coming to know him, the one who called us to himself by means of his marvelous glory and excellence."
~ 2 Peter 1:3 (NLT)

God is love! His unfailing love for us provides both the physical things we need on a daily basis as well as spiritual gifts. Everything we have and are is because of His love.

EVERY BREATH WE DRAW IS A GIFT OF HIS LOVE, EVERY MOMENT OF EXISTENCE IS A GRACE, FOR IT BRINGS WITH IT IMMENSE GRACES FROM HIM.

Have you considered that your life and each breath are because of God's great love, grace and goodness for you?

> *"But because of his great love for us, God, who is rich in mercy, made us alive with Christ even when we were dead in transgressions—it is by grace you have been saved."*
> ~ Ephesians 2:4-5

Even though we were born into sin through Adam and Eve, God's love, mercy, and grace triumph. God's grace saves us from our transgressions. What a privilege every breath we take is. We show our gratitude through the way we live our lives.

GRATITUDE THEREFORE TAKES NOTHING FOR GRANTED, IS NEVER UNRESPONSIVE, IS CONSTANTLY AWAKENING TO NEW WONDER AND TO PRAISE OF THE GOODNESS OF GOD.

Isn't it true that when we are filled with gratitude, we are deeply connected to the wonder and praise of our good, good God?

> *"I will remember the deeds of the Lord; yes, I will remember your wonders of old. I will ponder all your work, and meditate on your mighty deeds. Your way, O God, is holy. What god is great like our God? You are the God who works wonders; you have made known your might among the peoples."*
> ~ Psalm 77:11-14 (ESV)

When we take time to reflect on the many ways the Lord is continually working in our lives, revealing His presence and love in deed and the orchestrations of our steps, it is easy to see His goodness. Each day gives us many reasons to be in awe of God and praise Him for His goodness. What gratitude fills our hearts.

FOR THE GRATEFUL PERSON KNOWS THAT GOD IS GOOD, NOT BY HEARSAY BUT BY EXPERIENCE. AND THAT IS WHAT MAKES ALL THE DIFFERENCE.

In your daily walk, do you personally experience the goodness of God that fills you with gratitude?

> *"What shall I return to the Lord for all his goodness to me? I will lift up the cup of salvation and call on the name of the Lord. I will fulfill my vows to the Lord in the presence of all his people."*
> ~ Psalm 116:12-14

When we personally experience the daily moments of seeing how good God is, our hearts and lives are filled with gratitude. Thanksgiving and praise are two ways we can express our gratitude to God.

Be encouraged to be grateful…

recognizing the love of God in everything He has given you.
for each breath you take, which is full of God's grace.
not taking anything for granted, but rather praising God for His goodness.
as you daily experience God's goodness.

REFLECTION:

Have you pondered how the Love of God is in everything?
How can you show gratitude to God for the gift of His grace?

> *"I always thank my God for you because of his grace given you in Christ Jesus."*
> ~ 1 Corinthians 1:4

Section 2

GOD'S GRACE MANIFESTED THROUGH THE SPIRIT

"But—when God our Savior revealed his kindness and love, he saved us, not because of the righteous things we had done, but because of his mercy. He washed away our sins, giving us a new birth and new life through the Holy Spirit. He generously poured out the Spirit upon us through Jesus Christ our Savior. Because of his grace he made us right in his sight and gave us confidence that we will inherit eternal life."
~ Titus 3:4-7 (NLT)

What wondrous love God has for each one of us! His mercy saves us from the unrighteousness we deserve. Because God sent Jesus to earth to take on the yoke of our sins by dying on the cross, we have access to the Holy Spirit, who gives us grace and makes us restored and assured of eternal life.

God's grace isn't necessarily a thing; it's a person—the Spirit! The Spirit leads us, provides strength, and helps sustain us in difficulties.

God's grace manifested through the Spirit.

> **G**od's
> **R**iches
> **A**t
> **C**hrist's
> **E**xpense

28

Grace

*"Grace is the face
that love wears
when it meets imperfection."*
~ Joseph R. Cooke

God's grace is a free gift that makes us right in His eyes because of Jesus' death on the cross and resurrection. Jesus took the weight of all our sins to allow us to live in freedom. Once we place our faith in Jesus, we partake of the glorious gift of God's grace. We do nothing to earn this grace—Jesus did it all!

*"We are made right with God by placing our faith in Jesus Christ.
And this is true for everyone who believes, no matter who we are.
For everyone has sinned; we all fall short of God's glorious standard.
Yet God, in his grace, freely makes us right in his sight. He did this
through Christ Jesus when he freed us from the penalty for our sins."*
~ Romans 3:22-24 (NLT)

*"Yes, God is more than ready to overwhelm you with every
form of grace, so that you will have more than enough of
everything—every moment and in every way. He will make
you overflow with abundance in every good thing you do."*
~ 2 Corinthians 9:8 (TPT)

Paul tells us that it is God's grace that equips us with all we need to be able to do good things because of Him. This grace will provide the strength, courage, and words to share God's goodness with others when we need it.

It empowers us to be Christ-like by sharing kindness, generosity, and compassion with others. All the good that we share is a result of God's grace.

What a gift God's grace is. We are made right with Him because of Jesus, and then God continues to give us grace to live righteous lives so we can share abundantly what we have been given. It is important to treat ourselves with grace too—with kindness, self-compassion, understanding, and respect.

In thinking of the sacrifice of Jesus, I interpret the above quote like this:

"Grace is the face
That JESUS (love) wears
When it meets OUR SINS (imperfection.)"
~ Joseph R. Cooke

God's grace provides us with the opportunity of a free, unmerited gift of Jesus shedding His blood for our sins. Jesus was obedient to God because of His love for God and for us. Jesus experienced God's grace, providing Him the courage, strength, and willingness to suffer a brutal death so we can spend eternity in their presence.

"This is my commandment: Love each other in the same way I have loved
you. There is no greater love than to lay down one's life for one's friends."
~ John 15:12-13 (NLT)

Scripture says there is no greater love than to lay down our life for others. Jesus did this with His own life. May it touch your spirit to know how loved you are.

"Two others, both criminals, were led out to be executed with him.
When they came to a place called The Skull, they nailed him to the cross.
And the criminals were also crucified—one on his right and one on his

left. Jesus said, 'Father, forgive them, for they don't know what they are
doing.' And the soldiers gambled for his clothes by throwing dice."
~ Luke 23:32-34 (NLT)

Jesus, though innocent of any crime, was put to death as criminals were. Despite all the hardship, punishment, and beatings Jesus endured, He asked God to forgive them. He did not despise them or say a bad word to them.

"Jesus knew that his mission was now finished, and to fulfill
Scripture he said, 'I am thirsty.' A jar of sour wine was sitting
there, so they soaked a sponge in it, put it on a hyssop branch,
and held it up to his lips. When Jesus had tasted it, he said, 'It is
finished!' Then he bowed his head and gave up his spirit."
~ John 19:28-30 (NLT)

"It is finished!" What powerful words as Jesus took His last breath. That final step when God's grace was made available for all humankind. Jesus met and redeemed our sinful nature, our imperfection because of Adam and Eve's sin of eating from the Tree of Life.

What a beautiful acrostic for the word grace:

<u>G</u>od's
<u>R</u>iches
<u>A</u>t
<u>C</u>hrist's
<u>E</u>xpense

In thinking of us, I interpret the quote like this:

"Grace is the face
That love (Jesus in us) wears
When it meets imperfection (in others or ourselves.)"
~ Joseph R. Cooke

"For the grace of God has appeared that offers salvation to all people. It teaches us to say 'No' to ungodliness and worldly passions, and to live self-controlled, upright and godly lives in this present age, while we wait for the blessed hope—the appearing of the glory of our great God and Savior, Jesus Christ, who gave himself for us to redeem us from all wickedness and to purify for himself a people that are his very own, eager to do what is good."
~ Titus 2:11-14

Because of God's grace, freely given, we are able to share that grace with others and ourselves. Grace gives us the ability to live godly lives, being self-controlled, righteous people who share kindness and forgiveness. We should neither be judgmental nor condemning.

Be encouraged to…

> reflect on and thank God for His grace.
> write a heartfelt letter to Jesus thanking Him for His love and sacrifice for you.
> let Jesus' love flow from your actions.
> practice extending acts of grace to others and especially yourself.

REFLECTION:

When did you see God's grace shine forth?
How can you grant yourself some of God's grace?

"You then, my child, be strengthened by the grace that is in Christ Jesus."
~ 2 Timothy 2:1 (ESV)

Christine M. Fisher

29

Thin Places

"Thin places"—a new term I recently heard and found interesting. It is a concept in Celtic Christian spirituality, with one explanation of it being **a time where the space (veil) between heaven and earth grows thin and we encounter the sacred.** We can see with our hearts God's divine orchestrations. We can also view "thin places" as moments of grace that renew us.

"We are living in a world
that is absolutely transparent,
and God is shining
through all the time."
~ Thomas Merton

I have gratitude for experiencing "thin places." When I see God at work, it strengthens my faith and reminds me how much He loves us.

"Jacob left Beersheba and set out for Harran. When he reached a certain place, he stopped for the night because the sun had set. Taking one of the stones there, he put it under his head and lay down to sleep. He had a dream in which he saw a stairway resting on the earth, with its top reaching to heaven, and the angels of God were ascending and descending on it. There above it stood the Lord, and he said: 'I am the Lord, the God of your father Abraham and the God of Isaac. I will give you and your descendants the land on which you are lying. Your descendants will be like the dust of the earth, and you will spread out to the west and to the east, to the north and to the south. All peoples on earth will be blessed through you and your offspring. I am with you and

*will watch over you wherever you go, and I will bring you back to this
land. I will not leave you until I have done what I have promised you.'*

*"When Jacob awoke from his sleep, he thought, 'Surely the
Lord is in this place, and I was not aware of it.' He was
afraid and said, 'How awesome is this place! This is none
other than the house of God; this is the gate of heaven.'"*
~ Genesis 28:10-17

Jacob's dream bears some credibility to knowing that heaven and earth do
meet, even in our humanity. God walks with us, watches over us, and wants
only the best for us. This dream brought Jacob to the awareness to look for
and see how God is always with us. He, too, rejoices in God's goodness.

I participated in a two-day celebration with friends to honor the heavenly
birthday of another friend who died. A few friends and I went to coffee
rather than stay at a luncheon at church. After coffee, I saw that the church
celebration was wrapping up, and I was able to grab some food. As I ate,
a lady came up to me and asked if I was an author. It began a beautiful
conversation as she shared how meaningful my book has been to her. I
couldn't help but give her a hug and let her know how that encouraged
me. Hearing this lady share how God is using the book for His glory was a
"thin place" for me—seeing how God inspired me to go back to the church
and orchestrated that encounter.

After the events of the weekend, I went to the cemetery where my friend
is buried. Ironically, I stopped the night before, but the gates were locked
for the day. This day I was there about five minutes before a truck pulled
up nearby and a gentleman came to the same spot I was. What are the
chances two of us were there for the same person at the same time—all
because of God's providence? I was curious to find out his connection, so
what a beautiful "thin place" it was sharing our stories of the impact our
deceased friend had on our lives.

My story with the deceased person was that he wanted to meet me after reading an article in the diocesan newspaper about my first book. So I meekly asked this new man if he would be interested in a book. He enthusiastically said yes and picked one out. It made me smile as our deceased friend was a big promoter of my books sharing them with others. This moment in time did indeed seem, almost literally, like heaven and earth met!

Be encouraged to…

> see what beautiful "thin places" God orchestrates.
> be open to seeking new places to experience God's presence.
> reflect on what places are "thin places" for you.
> share how God is shining through in your life.

REFLECTION:

What "thin places" do you frequent?
What is the last "thin place" event you experienced?

> *"The Word became flesh and made his dwelling among us.*
> *We have seen his glory, the glory of the one and only Son,*
> *who came from the Father, full of grace and truth."*
> ~ John 1:14

30

Divine

*"It's in the ordinary
we see the divine."*

Merriam-Webster.com defines "divine" as: "of, relating to, or proceeding directly from God." Do you agree that in the ordinary of life we see the divine? God takes the ordinary and the everyday things and transforms them by His presence and grace.

When God inspired me to start a website, the purpose was to highlight His presence in the ordinary of our lives. Putting my thoughts to the written word helps them stop from just running through my head.

> *"As Jesus was walking beside the Sea of Galilee, he saw two brothers, Simon called Peter and his brother Andrew. They were casting a net into the lake, for they were fishermen. 'Come, follow me,' Jesus said, 'and I will send you out to fish for people.' At once they left their nets and followed him. Going on from there, he saw two other brothers, James son of Zebedee and his brother John. They were in a boat with their father Zebedee, preparing their nets. Jesus called them, and immediately they left the boat and their father and followed him."*
> ~ Matthew 4:18-22

How interesting to see that Jesus, both divine and human, called as His first followers simple, ordinary men who were fishermen. These men, who became known as His disciples, met the divine in the ordinariness of their life of being fishermen. We too have opportunities when the divine meets us in the ordinary of our lives.

Christine M. Fisher

"Now he [Jesus] had to go through Samaria. So he came to a town in Samaria called Sychar, near the plot of ground Jacob had given to his son Joseph. Jacob's well was there, and Jesus, tired as he was from the journey, sat down by the well. It was about noon. When a Samaritan woman came to draw water, Jesus said to her, 'Will you give me a drink?' (His disciples had gone into the town to buy food.) The Samaritan woman said to him, 'You are a Jew and I am a Samaritan woman. How can you ask me for a drink?' (For Jews do not associate with Samaritans.) Jesus answered her, 'If you knew the gift of God and who it is that asks you for a drink, you would have asked him and he would have given you living water.' The woman said, 'I know that Messiah' (called Christ) 'is coming. When he comes, he will explain everything to us.' Then Jesus declared, 'I, the one speaking to you—I am he.'"
~ John 4:4-10, 25-26

Jesus is always working out divine orchestrations. This Samaritan woman was doing the ordinary task of getting water from the town well when she had a face-to-face encounter that changed her life forever. She encountered the Messiah who loved her despite living a sinful life—so much so that she changed her life from that day forward. Jesus is always waiting to encounter us in the ordinary circumstances of our lives.

These people had the distinct privilege of being alive at the same time as Jesus walked this earth—of meeting the divine in person. How fortunate we are to be alive in this day and age, having the Holy Spirit to guide and lead us—thus having the opportunity of meeting the divine every day in our lives.

What are some ways we see the divine in the ordinary of our lives?

The chance encounter of running into people we haven't seen in a long time.

Seeing miracles happen before our eyes, like someone having a feeding tube for eight months and suddenly being able to swallow again or giving parents the strength to care for a physically challenged child in their home.

Observing a total solar eclipse with God's perfect timing in providing a break in the clouds.

The miracle of new life, whether people, animals, or flowers.

Someone turning their life over to Jesus.

Seeing a special reminder of God's love in our lives such as hearts, rainbows, or cloud shapes.

In receiving an unexpected hug from a toddler.

Looking into the eyes of a person near death.

When experiencing a sunrise or sunset.

Soaking in the view of a vast ocean.

In having clean water to drink and bathe with.

When standing in faith in prayer with other people.

How can we be more open to seeing the divine in the ordinary?

Starting each day with gratitude for waking up to a new day.

Asking God to help you see His presence in the little details.

Being totally present in the moments with other people.

Giving thanks to God throughout the day for being in control of life.

Reflecting on God's goodness that we see throughout the day.

"There is something holy,
something divine hidden
in the most ordinary situations,
and it is up to each one of you to discover it."
~ St. Josemaria Escriva

Be encouraged to…

      be more aware of the divine meeting with the daily ordinary events
      of life.
      see the presence of the divine each day.
      seek the divine's assistance in a difficult situation.
      pray to see the divine in all of humanity, even those who hurt you.

REFLECTION:

When did you see the divine show up to help you through a negative circumstance?
How have you experienced the divine with another person?

"Grace and peace be yours in abundance through the knowledge of God and of Jesus our Lord. His divine power has given us everything we need for a godly life through our knowledge of him who called us by his own glory and goodness. Through these he has given us his very great and precious promises, so that through them you may participate in the divine nature, having escaped the corruption in the world caused by evil desires."
~ 2 Peter 1:2-4

31

Forgiveness

As gazed out on the vastness of calm Lake Ontario, feeling oneness with the gentle, rolling waves, I read this Scripture.

> *"Who is a God like you, who pardons sin and forgives the transgression of the remnant of his inheritance? You do not stay angry forever but delight to show mercy. You will again have compassion on us; you will tread our sins underfoot and hurl all our iniquities into the depths of the sea."*
> ~ Micah 7:18-19

God is great and loves us so much. Even when we, like Israel from this Scripture, grumble, complain, and get angry with God, He does not remain angry with us. Instead, God lavishes us with His mercy, compassion, and grace. I could envision God stomping on, and then hurling the evil we do out into the depths of the water. The vastness of the water lets us know God remembers our sins no more. The gentle waves reminded me of His compassion and mercy washing over us.

God's mercy and forgiveness are beautiful gifts of His grace. Once we accept Jesus as our Lord and Savior and repent of our sins, grace becomes a part of our lives. God sent His only Son, Jesus, into the world to die for our sins.

Since we are made in God's image, we also have the responsibility to extend His mercy, compassion, and grace to others, especially those who have sinned against us. He has buried the sins in the depths of the sea and completely forgiven us. Can we do the same?

Christine M. Fisher

What are some verses of encouragement for us to forgive others?

"Therefore, as God's chosen people, holy and dearly loved, clothe yourselves with compassion, kindness, humility, gentleness and patience. Bear with each other and forgive one another if any of you has a grievance against someone. Forgive as the Lord forgave you. And over all these virtues put on love, which binds them all together in perfect unity."
~ Colossians 3:12-14

Paul, in his letter to the Colossians, encourages us to live as God's chosen people. Our lives should emulate God's compassion, kindness, humility, gentleness, patience, forgiveness, and love, which unite us all. He specifically reminds us to forgive those who trespass against us in the same way that God forgives us.

"Instead, be kind to each other, tenderhearted, forgiving one another, just as God through Christ has forgiven you. Imitate God, therefore, in everything you do, because you are his dear children. Live a life filled with love, following the example of Christ. He loved us and offered himself as a sacrifice for us, a pleasing aroma to God."
~ Ephesians 4:32-5:2 (NLT)

Paul reminds the Christians in Ephesus how to live: being kind, tenderhearted, forgiving, and loving in the same way that Christ modeled. Once again, he emphasizes how God, by sending Jesus to suffer and die for our sins, has forgiven them. Christ sacrificed His very life to set us free; it was a mighty act of unconditional love that we need to share with others.

"Then Peter came to Jesus and asked, 'Lord, how many times shall I forgive my brother or sister who sins against me? Up to seven times?' Jesus answered, 'I tell you, not seven times, but seventy-seven times.'"
~ Matthew 18:21-22

In this Scripture, Peter, one of Jesus' original disciples, was ready to forgive others who have wronged him up to seven times. Jesus' response of not seven but seventy-seven times shows to what lengths He goes to forgive us. We need to extend that same sincerity of love and forgiveness from our hearts to others as we try to imitate what we have received from God.

Be encouraged to…

> live sincerely knowing God has hurled your sins into the depths of the sea.
> forgive others as God has forgiven you.
> let your life be your offering of sacrifice to God.
> ask for help to forgive others sincerely from your heart.

REFLECTION:

Who has hurt you that you need to forgive with God's grace?
Do you need to be more like God and remember no more the wrong you did once you repented?

> *"In him we have redemption through his blood, the forgiveness*
> *of our trespasses, according to the riches of his grace, which*
> *he lavished upon us, in all wisdom and insight."*
> ~ Ephesians 1:7-8 (ESV)

32

Engulfed In Deep Waters

How I relish being engulfed in God's presence and love while vacationing on Lake Ontario, where the beauty of God's creation is endless. On this visit, Lake Ontario sounded like a mighty ocean as the wind made the waves the highest and most violent I've seen there. It never ceases to amaze me how God made this lake to sometimes be as still and calm as a sheet of glass and other times a sea of endless, tumultuous waves.

It is beautiful to experience both and see how God is present in both. Isn't that the perfect parallel with our lives? God is present with us each moment, in both the difficult storms and in the peaceful, calm times.

Being mesmerized watching and listening to the huge waves, the themes of "engulfed" and "deep waters" came to mind. I also reflected on the wind, reminding me of the Holy Spirit's presence as I watched the water. What could God be showing my spirit? Despite the scene in front of me, I felt peace. It was soothing despite the chaos of the waters.

I enjoyed taking time to research different Bible verses that use the themes of "engulfed" and "deep waters."

> "But now, O Jacob, listen to the Lord who created you. O Israel, the one who formed you says, 'Do not be afraid, for I have ransomed you. I have called you by name; you are mine. When you go through deep waters, I will be with you. When you go through rivers of difficulty, you will not drown. When you walk through the fire of oppression, you will not be burned up; the flames will not consume you.'"
> ~ Isaiah 43:1-2 (NLT)

God lets us know that He calls us by name because we belong to Him, and we are His chosen ones who need not be afraid of the deep waters. He is always with us through the storms and the rivers of difficulty. Because of this, we will not drown. The deep waters that engulf us and the flames of oppression will not prevail. God's presence, love, and grace are greater.

REFLECTION:

When have you felt the Lord call your name, knowing you are His chosen one?
When did you reach out to grab God's hand to pull you out of the deep waters?

> *"From inside the fish Jonah prayed to the Lord his God. He said: 'In my distress I called to the Lord, and he answered me. From deep in the realm of the dead I called for help, and you listened to my cry. You hurled me into the depths, into the very heart of the seas, and the currents swirled about me; all your waves and breakers swept over me. I said, I have been banished from your sight; yet I will look again toward your holy temple. The engulfing waters threatened me, the deep surrounded me; seaweed was wrapped around my head. To the roots of the mountains I sank down; the earth beneath barred me in forever. But you, Lord my God, brought my life up from the pit. When my life was ebbing away, I remembered you, Lord, and my prayer rose to you, to your holy temple. Those who cling to worthless idols turn away from God's love for them. But I, with shouts of grateful praise, will sacrifice to you. What I have vowed I will make good. I will say, Salvation comes from the Lord.' And the Lord commanded the fish, and it vomited Jonah onto dry land."*
>
> ~ Jonah 2:1-10

Jonah knew the Lord had called him to go to Nineveh to preach against the wickedness of the city yet chose to run. God sent a great wind and violent storm upon the sea, and Jonah knew that for the storm to subside, he needed to be thrown overboard. God provided for Jonah's safety by providing a fish to swallow him where he remained for three days and three nights. Jonah realized the error of his ways and the sovereignty of God.

Isn't Jonah's description of the sea one you can relate to?
Does your life ever fit that description of the sea?
Currents swirling all about you, the waves and breakers of life sweeping over you, the waters engulfing you, being out in deep waters, and seaweed wrapped around you?
Doesn't your life feel like it is ebbing away at times?

What lessons does Jonah give us for these times?

To remember...

that God is always with us.
to pray to God for help.
to turn from idols.
to be obedient to Him.
to offer sacrifices of praise to God, for our salvation is from Him.

REFLECTION:

When have you felt like Jonah in the stormy sea?
What helps you to overcome the storms?

"Then he got into the boat and his disciples followed him. Suddenly a furious storm came up on the lake, so that the waves swept over the boat. But Jesus was sleeping. The disciples went and woke him, saying, 'Lord, save us! We're going to drown!' He replied, 'You of little faith, why are you so afraid?' Then he got up and rebuked the winds and the waves, and it was completely calm. The men were amazed and asked, 'What kind of man is this? Even the winds and the waves obey him!'"
~ Matthew 8:23-27

When a violent storm whose waves are so high that the boat takes on water, the disciples are scared and afraid, especially with Jesus sleeping. In their panic, they awakened Jesus, who rebuked the winds and waves. Jesus asks them why they were fearful instead of holding on to their faith.

REFLECTION:

In what storm in your life did you not have faith that God was in charge? Have you failed to see Jesus in the boat with you?

Be encouraged to…

> know you are God's chosen one.
> experience God with you in the deep waters.
> be obedient to God's call.
> know God will get you through the storm.
> replace fear with faith and know that God is in charge.
> call out to God to rebuke the wind and waves in your life.

"He prayed to the Lord, 'Isn't this what I said, Lord, when I was still at home? That is what I tried to forestall by fleeing to Tarshish. I knew that you are a gracious and compassionate God, slow to anger and abounding in love, a God who relents from sending calamity.'"
~ Jonah 4:2

33

Deep Calls to Deep

As I soaked up the beauty of Lake Ontario, with the forceful wind making the waves even deeper, I was reminded of the phrase "deep calls to deep."

"Why, my soul, are you downcast?
Why so disturbed within me?
Put your hope in God,
for I will yet praise him,
my Savior and my God.
My soul is downcast within me;
therefore I will remember you
from the land of the Jordan,
the heights of Hermon—from Mount Mizar.
Deep calls to deep
in the roar of your waterfalls;
all your waves and breakers
have swept over me.
By day the Lord directs his love,
at night his song is with me—
a prayer to the God of my life."
~ Psalm 42:5-8

The Psalmist's soul is downcast, but he knows hope is found in God, and continues to praise Him, even in the pain. While remembering God's faithfulness in providing and His love that is always with him, he knows he will make it through the deep waters.

Do you need that powerful reminder too?

I see two main ways to view this particular verse:

> *"Deep calls to deep*
> *in the roar of your waterfalls;*
> *all your waves and breakers*
> *have swept over me."*

It is a cry from the heart when we go through troubled times.

During the deep, rough waters of life, when the waves and breakers cover us, we can cry out to God and know He is with us. He will never leave us. Our deepest needs are met with God's all-sufficient presence and help.

It is a call to deep intimacy with God, where spirit meets spirit.

God made us to have a deep desire for Him. It is the "hole" or emptiness we feel in our hearts until we come to Christ. Our faith usually starts in our heads but needs to move to our hearts. As God takes possession of our hearts, we are called into deeper and deeper intimacy with Him. It is more of a spirit connection. Words might even be replaced with a oneness with Him. God often calls us to go deeper in relationship with Him as He helps us face different things that might need exploring in our lives.

What is the "deep" in your life that God is calling you to face?

To forgive yourself for past mistakes and hurts?
> To enter into a more personal relationship with Him?
>> To have total trust in Him to provide what you need at the perfect time?

I pray that God will help you face the deep in your life as you step out in faith to take His hand. The waves and breakers of His peace, love, joy, comfort, and presence will engulf you in the deep waters. Know that God is mightier than the deep waves and breakers of the waterfalls in our lives. As you face the deep in your life, may you experience the deepness of perfect unity with God's presence all the way to the core of your being.

Be encouraged to experience...

> God with you in the deep waters of life.
> God calling you to go deeper in intimacy with Him.
> God being mightier than the waves and breakers of the waterfalls of life.

REFLECTION:

What deep water has God helped you through?
What deep water do you need to face with God's help?

> *"He has caused his wondrous works to be remembered;*
> *the Lord is gracious and merciful."*
> - Psalm 111:4 (ESV)

34

A Powerful Prayer

I can't.

      You can.

            You promised.

                  Please do.

I CAN'T.

"When he had finished speaking, he said to Simon, 'Put out into deep water, and let down the nets for a catch.' Simon answered, 'Master, we've worked hard all night and haven't caught anything. But because you say so, I will let down the nets.' When they had done so, they caught such a large number of fish that their nets began to break."

~ Luke 5:4-6

Despite being fishermen all their lives and knowing the water, the disciples did not have any luck catching fish this particular night. Jesus told them where to again lower their nets, and they were quickly filled to the breaking point with fish. It is the power from above that produces abundance in our lives. We cannot boast about ourselves, as we do not have the power.

YOU CAN.

"God can do anything, you know—far more than you could ever imagine or guess or request in your wildest dreams! He does it not by pushing us around but by working within us, his Spirit deeply and gently within

            Christine M. Fisher

us. Glory to God in the church! Glory to God in the Messiah, in Jesus!
Glory down all the generations! Glory through all millennia! Oh, yes!"
~ Ephesians 3:20-21 (MSG)

God can do anything. He makes everything work together. When we get to heaven, maybe we will realize even more the goodness He has bestowed upon us. In the meantime, our faith helps us believe and know that with God, nothing is impossible.

YOU PROMISED.

"For God so loved the world that he gave his one and only Son, that
whoever believes in him shall not perish but have eternal life."
~ John 3:16

God loves us so much that He sent Jesus to save us from our sins. Because of Jesus, we can have eternal life. What a beautiful promise.

"If we confess our sins, he is faithful and just and will forgive
us our sins and purify us from all unrighteousness."
~ 1 John 1:9

God promised that our sins would be forgiven, and we are declared righteous in His eyes. It is all because Jesus took our sins upon His shoulders and died on the cross.

"When you pass through the waters, I will be with you; and when you pass
through the rivers, they will not sweep over you. When you walk through
the fire, you will not be burned; the flames will not set you ablaze."
~ Isaiah 43:2

When it feels like we are in the raging waters or in the flames of fire of difficult circumstances, we are assured that God is with us, providing for us, keeping us safe.

Please do.

"But blessed are your eyes because they see, and your ears because they hear. For truly I tell you, many prophets and righteous people longed to see what you see but did not see it, and to hear what you hear but did not hear it."
~ Matthew 13:16-17

God follows through on His promises. We ask for spiritual eyes and ears to see and hear how He fulfills them in our lives. May we live in joyful expectation to see how God is working to fulfill His glorious promises and sovereignty.

My friend who shared this prayer uses it in this way. If he is praying for Susan to come back to the Lord, he says:

I can't... move Susan's heart to love you, Jesus.

    You can... soften her heart to be aware of you, Jesus.

        You promised... to open the eyes of our hearts and pursue us with relentless love.

            Please do... as Susan needs to know you are merciful and loving.

Be encouraged to...

    repeat the simple prayer often.

    know the power from above produces abundance.

    see how God can do anything.

    reflect on the truth of God's promises.

    put on your spiritual eyes and ears to experience God working in our lives.

    pray this prayer for specific people and requests.

Christine M. Fisher

REFLECTION:

Do you need to focus more on what God can do?
Which of God's promises do you need to be reminded of most?

> *"Therefore the Lord waits to be gracious to you, and therefore he exalts himself to show mercy to you. For the Lord is a God of justice; blessed are all those who wait for him."*
> ~ Isaiah 30:18 (ESV)

35

Loincloth Lessons

"This is what the Lord said to me: 'Go and buy a linen loincloth and put it on, but do not wash it.' So I bought the loincloth as the Lord directed me, and I put it on. Then the Lord gave me another message, 'Take the linen loincloth you are wearing, and go to the Euphrates River. Hide it there in a hole in the rocks.' So I went and hid it by the Euphrates as the Lord had instructed me.

"A long time afterward the Lord said to me, 'Go back to the Euphrates and get the loincloth I told you to hide there.' So I went to the Euphrates and dug it out of the hole where I had hidden it. But now it was rotting and falling apart. The loincloth was good for nothing.

"Then I received this message from the Lord: 'This is what the Lord says: This shows how I will rot away the pride of Judah and Jerusalem. These wicked people refuse to listen to me. They stubbornly follow their own desires and worship other gods. Therefore, they will become like this loincloth—good for nothing! As a loincloth clings to a man's waist, so I created Judah and Israel to cling to me, says the Lord. They were to be my people, my pride, my glory—an honor to my name. But they would not listen to me.'"
~ Jeremiah 13:1-11 (NLT)

We know God made a covenant with the people of Israel at Sinai, the chosen people He picked to bring the good news to all nations. The covenant was that they were to be obedient to Him and He would continue to bless them. God protected the people from Egypt but they were not obedient to Him, so for hundreds of years, God dealt with them by sending curses to them. This passage is the Lord's message to the prophet Jeremiah sharing His frustration about Israel. We see how Jeremiah has a heart willing to listen to God and to walk in obedience.

What are three main things we can learn from this passage?

THE LORD HAS A SENSE OF HUMOR AND CAN USE ANYTHING TO TEACH US LESSONS.

God used the loincloth to get our attention and teach us about the intimate relationship He wants with us. First Jeremiah is told by God to buy the linen loincloth, put it on, then go to the Euphrates River, take it off, and hide it in a hole in the rocks. At the proper time appointed by God, Jeremiah returned to collect the loincloth to find it had rotted and was no longer usable. God's lesson is if Israel continued in their ways, they would be good for nothing.

THE LORD DOES NOT TOLERATE PRIDE.

God was teaching us that just as the loincloth had rotted away when Jeremiah was told to retrieve it, God had the power to rot away the pride of Israel. When our pride gets in the way, we tend to not listen to what God is telling us; we want to do our own thing, and we might start worshipping false gods.

THE LORD WANTS US TO CLING TO HIM ALONE.

There is nothing closer to us than a loincloth, aka underwear! God wants to be that intimate with us. Just as He told Jeremiah, we were created to cling to Him. With the symbolism of the loincloth, we know God is always with us and clings to our every movement. We are God's people, His pride, His glory, and an honor to His name.

God goes to great lengths to get our attention and nothing can stop us from His great love.

Be encouraged to…

> be obedient to God's call.
> see God's sense of humor.
> break down the barriers of pride.
> give glory and praise to God.
> cling to God and Him alone.
> know that God is closer to you than a loincloth.

REFLECTION:

What lesson from the loincloth do you need to work on most?
How have you seen the Lord use a sense of humor to teach you a lesson?

> *"May the grace of the Lord Jesus be with God's holy people."*
> ~ Revelation 22:21 (NLT)

36

Lay Down Crosses

Crosses are a normal occurrence in life. Jesus, both divine and human, carried and suffered upon a cross in His humanity. His cross was both physical and figurative as He carried the weight of our sins on His shoulders.

"Finally Pilate handed him [Jesus] over to them to be crucified. So the soldiers took charge of Jesus. Carrying his own cross, he went out to the place of the Skull (which in Aramaic is called Golgotha). There they crucified him, and with him two others—one on each side and Jesus in the middle."
~ John 19:16-18

"As the soldiers led him [Jesus] away, they seized Simon from Cyrene, who was on his way in from the country, and put the cross on him and made him carry it behind Jesus."
~ Luke 23:26

As Jesus began to carry His physical cross, how unexpectedly that Simon from Cyrene was forced to help carry the cross. It shows the importance of others being instrumental in helping us carry our crosses—being there for one another.

Most of our crosses do not require us to lay down our lives like Jesus did. But with Jesus willingly suffering death on a cross to set us free, how much more should we accept our crosses?

"From that time on Jesus began to explain to his disciples that he must go to Jerusalem and suffer many things at the hands of the elders, the chief priests and the teachers of the law, and that he must be killed and on the

third day be raised to life. Peter took him aside and began to rebuke him.
'Never, Lord!' he said. 'This shall never happen to you!' Jesus turned and
said to Peter, 'Get behind me, Satan! You are a stumbling block to me; you
do not have in mind the concerns of God, but merely human concerns.'
Then Jesus said to his disciples, 'Whoever wants to be my disciple must deny
themselves and take up their cross and follow me. For whoever wants to
save their life will lose it, but whoever loses their life for me will find it.'"
~ Matthew 16:21-25

When Jesus shared about His approaching suffering and means of death, Peter did not want to hear it. Jesus pointed out that suffering has an eternal consequence, and that is what is most important. We shouldn't be as concerned with the human part of suffering. Just as Jesus denied Himself, offering His life for us and taking up His cross with dignity, so Jesus instructs us to do the same. We will find our true life in Him.

What can we do when our crosses seem too heavy for us to bear?

> Be honest with the Lord acknowledging what our crosses are rather than ignoring them.
> Accept our crosses knowing God is with us rather than being resentful and angry.
> Lay down our crosses at the foot of the cross as we pour our hearts out to Him.
> Surrender our will to God, knowing He is sovereign.
> See if we can change something to help alleviate the crosses.
> If we can't change the situation, offer the cross up as a sacrifice for someone.
> Share the cross with a trusted friend who can stand in prayer and faith with us as sometimes we need a human too.

I know of a local family who is dealing with a major cross. Remi, their oldest child, found out he had a sizeable brain tumor. He had surgery, chemo, and radiation. We are praising the Lord that the pathology report was MUCH better than anticipated, and doctors are giving him a 90-98% success rate.

I am in awe of the faith of young Remi and his family. Right before his surgery, Remi said,

> *"God is good.*
> *One hard thing at a time."*
> ~ Remi, 11 years old

What stellar faith from an eleven-year-old and a great reminder for us all!

> *"Lord, our Lord, how majestic is your name in all the earth!*
> *You have set your glory in the heavens. Through the praise*
> *of children and infants you have established a stronghold*
> *against your enemies, to silence the foe and the avenger."*
> ~ Psalm 8:1-2

It is a blessing to see a child step out in faith and praise the Lord, especially in the face of adversity. God says that the praise of children can silence the foe. I believe God will do this in Remi's life, because he sees God's glory that fills the earth and heaven.

> *"Taste and see that the Lord is good. Oh, the*
> *joys of those who take refuge in him!"*
> ~ Psalm 34:8 (NLT)

> *"For I can do everything through Christ, who gives me strength."*
> ~ Philippians 4:13 (NLT)

These two verses are what I see Remi living out. What beauty to see a young person of faith who already knows the goodness of God. Remi knows that Christ is with him and giving him strength to face one hard thing at a time.

The family's latest update said, "Remington IS in for a tough road, but we are taking one VICTORY at a time!"

Be encouraged to...

> lay down a cross at the foot of the cross.
> help carry a cross for someone who is heavily burdened.
> ask for strength to carry your crosses.
> see God's goodness as you take one hard thing at a time.
> dedicate the suffering of a cross to someone in need.
> know there is victory in the cross.

REFLECTION:

What cross are you ready to lay down at the foot of the cross?
Can you thank someone who has prayed you through a cross?

"I have been crucified with Christ and I no longer live, but Christ lives in me. The life I now live in the body, I live by faith in the Son of God, who loved me and gave himself for me. I do not set aside the grace of God, for if righteousness could be gained through the law, Christ died for nothing!"
~ Galatians 2:20-21

37

An Ocean of Love

Are you captivated when looking out on an ocean where it seems the water flows right into the horizon?

Isn't it mesmerizing to watch the waves and the tides?

Why can't we see the ocean's end?

Maybe God created it that way so we could marvel and be immersed in His awesomeness and His love.

I have always loved the ocean waters. My family would frequent North Wildwood, NJ, and I would be sad when it was time to leave. Perhaps it was because I experienced God's presence while gazing out on the ocean and thought He wasn't with me apart from the ocean.

This quote seems like the perfect analogy to help us reflect on God's love.

"God's love is like an ocean;
you can see its beginning
but not its end."
~ Rick Warren

God's love for us is grand.

God sent His only Son, Jesus, to die for our sins so that we have the privilege of spending eternity in heaven with Him.

Do we live each day realizing the vastness of God's love for us?

God's love is endless, just as we can't see the end of an ocean.

"'For the mountains may depart and the hills be removed, but my steadfast love shall not depart from you, and my covenant of peace shall not be removed,' says the Lord, who has compassion on you."
~ Isaiah 54:10 (ESV)

God's love for us is steadfast, which means it is not subject to ever change. He loves us regardless of what we have done or failed to do. God's love for each one of His children is unwavering and faithful. Even when we don't love or accept Him, God's love for us is never-ending. He always wants the best for us. Let that truth settle deep into your soul.

God's love is deeper than the deepest waters of an ocean.

"And may you have the power to understand, as all God's people should, how wide, how long, how high, and how deep his love is. May you experience the love of Christ, though it is too great to understand fully. Then you will be made complete with all the fullness of life and power that comes from God." ~ Ephesians 3:18-19 (NLT)

Paul prayed we may know in our hearts and experience how all-encompassing God's love truly is. He knows our finite minds can't quite fathom the deepness of it, but we can experience it on different levels as we see glimpses of His love when we see Him working in our lives. Our lives become richer when we live deeper in God's love.

God's love is always with us, even in the storms and when the ocean waves are in full force.

"When you go through deep waters, I will be with you. When you go through rivers of difficulty, you will not drown..."
~ Isaiah 43:2 (NLT)

Christine M. Fisher

God's love is so great, that even when the waves of deep trials try to overtake us, He assures us He will be with us. Even when the waves are higher than us, God will not let us drown. God is always with us, helping us through. What a wonderful God we have!

Be encouraged to…

> give thanks to God for His unwavering and faithful love.
> experience the deepness of God's love for you.
> reach out to God when you are in the deep waters.

REFLECTION:

When did you experience the depth of God's love for you?
What storm has God's love gotten you through?

"But God, being rich in mercy, because of the great love with which
he loved us, even when we were dead in our trespasses, made us
alive together with Christ—by grace you have been saved."
~ Ephesians 2:4-5 (ESV)

38

Crosses

Let's take a few minutes to reflect on Jesus' cross and the crosses we bear.

Think about Jesus' life. God sent Jesus to this earth to live in human form, so we can relate to Him and He to us.

> *"Therefore, since we have a great high priest who has ascended into heaven, Jesus the Son of God, let us hold firmly to the faith we profess. For we do not have a high priest who is unable to empathize with our weaknesses, but we have one who has been tempted in every way, just as we are—yet he did not sin."*
> ~ Hebrews 4:14-15

Jesus experienced what we do, with the exception of sin, because of His divinity. We have someone who understands and loves us unconditionally, despite our sinful nature. Jesus knows our weaknesses and wants us to hold onto Him to help us through life's trials.

God's plan for Jesus was to die a painful, brutal death, which was death on a cross.

> *"He committed no sin, and no deceit was found in his mouth. When they hurled their insults at him, he did not retaliate; when he suffered, he made no threats. Instead, he entrusted himself to him who judges justly. He himself bore our sins in his body on the cross, so that we might die to sins and live for righteousness; by his wounds you have been healed."*
> ~ 1 Peter 2:22-24

Christine M. Fisher

Without the cross, there would be no resurrection. Jesus willingly suffered a brutal beating and death on the cross to set all of humanity free. What a sacrifice of obedience to God and great love for us. The terrible events of Jesus on the cross would appear to be one of the worst things, but God allowed it, and from the cross would flow the greatest good ever to come to the world. God uses everything for His good and ours.

"As they led Jesus away, a man named Simon, who was from Cyrene, happened to be coming in from the countryside. The soldiers seized him and put the cross on him and made him carry it behind Jesus."
~ Luke 23:26 (NLT)

Our understanding is that Jesus' cross was probably between thirty and forty pounds. How fitting that the soldiers allowed someone to help Jesus carry His cross, most likely because He was physically exhausted from the beating. Imagine being Simon, probably on his way to the Passover Feast in Jerusalem, and being unexpectedly pulled from the crowd to help carry Jesus' cross. Notice that the passage says Simon *"carried it behind Jesus."* I think that is an important parallel with the crosses in our lives. Jesus is the one carrying the brunt of our crosses as we join Him. He is yoked to us in our suffering and has compassion for us.

Luke's version of the above verse ties in and takes on greater meaning when we read:

"Then he [Jesus] said to them all: 'Whoever wants to be my disciple must deny themselves and take up their cross daily and follow me.'"
~ Luke 9:23

Simon was privileged to put these words into action. Perhaps helping Jesus carry His cross made Simon follow Him both figuratively and spiritually. Simon had to deny whatever his plans were to help Jesus carry His cross. We, too, need to follow Jesus as we carry our crosses together.

May you spend some quiet time to reflect upon and walk with Jesus on His road to Calvary, where He won the victory over the cross. His love for you is so great that He sacrificed His very life for you!

Be encouraged to…

> share your weaknesses in conversation with Jesus.
> thank Jesus for giving His life on the cross for your sins.
> put yourself in Simon's footsteps, helping Jesus carry the cross.
> take up your crosses daily, following behind Jesus, who carries most of the weight.

REFLECTION:

Whose cross are you helping to carry?
What cross will you allow someone else to help carry with you and Jesus?

"For all have sinned and fall short of the glory of God, and all are justified freely by his grace through the redemption that came by Christ Jesus."
~ Romans 3:23-24

39

Celebrating God's Goodness

*"Great is the Lord and most worthy of praise; his greatness no one can
fathom. One generation commends your works to another; they tell of your
mighty acts. They speak of the glorious splendor of your majesty—and
I will meditate on your wonderful works. They tell of the power of your
awesome works—and I will proclaim your great deeds. They celebrate
your abundant goodness and joyfully sing of your righteousness."*
- Psalm 145:3-7

It is important to share and celebrate God's goodness with each other to
help build our faith.

*"For you have been my hope, Sovereign Lord, my confidence
since my youth. From birth I have relied on you; you brought
me forth from my mother's womb. I will ever praise you."*
- Psalm 71:5-6

I celebrate God's goodness, which has always given me a love for Him,
even as a child. In the last five years, that love has grown stronger and more
intimate. Seeing the beauty of the natural world has awed me and brought
me closer to God through writing about Him.

*"Publish his glorious deeds among the nations. Tell everyone
about the amazing things he does. Great is the Lord! He is
most worthy of praise! He is to be feared above all gods."*
- 1 Chronicles 16:24-25 (NLT)
- Psalm 96:3-4 (NLT)

God used the Christian band, Third Day, to inspire me to join social media, which is when I met some online Christian bloggers who wrote to share their faith. One person had started penning short daily reflections that helped to inspire me to see if I could write weekly inspiration. This person also gave me information on how to start a website. I remember stepping out in faith on September 5, 2014, publishing my first reflection—a "test" to see if God would provide weekly inspiration. As we know, God has been faithful.

God has taught me three main lessons throughout this time:

God provides.

> *"And my God will supply every need of yours according*
> *to his riches in glory in Christ Jesus."*
> ~ Philippians 4:19 (ESV)

I've grown in confidence and trust that God will provide inspiration each week as I seek to share His goodness. Some weeks are more challenging than others, when doubts arise, but God provides a level of peace in my spirit when it seems "right." I have learned to let go of some of the control that I think I have and put my faith into action.

God is always working in our lives, even though we don't see it.

> *"So, because Jesus was doing these things [healings] on the Sabbath, the*
> *Jewish leaders began to persecute him. In his defense Jesus said to them,*
> *'My Father is always at his work to this very day, and I too am working.'"*
> ~ John 5:16-17

Both God and Jesus are always at work in our lives, whether we see it or not. Through the first five years of writing, I always felt it was difficult to get people to take time and read each week. I had no idea God, working in my life, was orchestrating people to encourage me to publish a book. Publishing has led me to share my books with strangers I meet, which has provided a way for me to reach more people and help spread God's Word. Everything is in God's perfect timing, even if we are not aware.

God provides beautiful orchestrations.

"And we know that God causes everything to work together for the good of those who love God and are called according to his purpose for them."
~ Romans 8:28 (NLT)

God wants the best for us and provides meaningful orchestrations in our lives. He can even make good come from evil. Throughout the last ten years, I have been blessed to meet and learn many people's stories. The people I have encountered continue to inspire and encourage me as we journey together. Stepping out in faith to share a book with a stranger often leads to a deepening spiritual relationship.

What are some gifts God has provided these past ten years?

Bloggers-to inspire me to write and share information on starting a website.

Weekly inspiration-to share my heart and faith.

A small fan base of dedicated readers-provided inspiration to publish books.

Editors-to encourage me and improve my grammar.

Meeting an author/speaker from Texas in New York State-who sent me information on how to write a manuscript. When I had a first-pass one prepared, she started helping self-publish first-time authors and felt the Lord wanted her to work with me.

Money-God always providing enough to help fund the next book.

People sharing-how God used a reflection or books to encourage them.

Peace and joy-writing weekly about God.

Stranger to spiritual family to journey with-from sharing a book. *God's Love Illuminated*-received the Henri award at the Joy & Company Awards in the Non-Fiction: Victorious Living category.

Be encouraged to...

> celebrate a way you see God's goodness in your life.
> thank God for a need He provided.
> trust God is working on something in your life that you aren't aware of yet.
> wait with expectation to see God's beautiful orchestrations.

REFLECTION:

What great deed of God do you need to proclaim?
What orchestration did God provide that you noticed later?

> *"By God's grace and mighty power, I have been given the privilege of serving him by spreading this Good News."*
> ~ Ephesians 3:7 (NLT)

40

Holy Spirit Arrival

When I was recounting a "God moment" story to a friend, he shared his quote:

> *"I am often amazed*
> *and seldom surprised*
> *when the Holy Spirit arrives*
> *disguised as coincidence."*
> ~ Deacon Michael Carroll

Vocabulary.com defines "coincidence" as: "an event that might have been arranged although it was really accidental."

Would you agree that oftentimes people view coincidences as just random happenings? When the Holy Spirit is involved in any event, it is safe to say it's not just coincidence, it's providential.

> *"And I will ask the Father, and he will give you another Advocate,*
> *who will never leave you. He is the Holy Spirit, who leads*
> *into all truth. The world cannot receive him, because it isn't*
> *looking for him and doesn't recognize him. But you know him,*
> *because he lives with you now and later will be in you."*
> ~ John 14:16-17 (NLT)

Jesus, knowing that soon He would be put to death, spoke these words of comfort and encouragement to His disciples so they knew they would never be left alone. What a great passage showing the intertwining relationship between God, Jesus, and the Holy Spirit—three in one. Jesus clearly says the world will not recognize the Holy Spirit's presence, only those who believe, which includes you and me.

"Commit to the Lord whatever you do, and he will establish your plans. The Lord works out everything to its proper end—even the wicked for a day of disaster."
~ Proverbs 16:3-4

When we commit all we do to the Lord, the Spirit takes over, leading and guiding us. He works everything out in His perfect way as we continue to walk in faith and trust. And the Spirit can make good out of our choices.

Do you often see the Holy Spirit arriving, disguised as coincidences that happen almost daily? Nothing in our lives happens by chance or by accident. God is always working His plans out.

Recently, I saw the Holy Spirit arrive in my life, providing two encounters with people. The Holy Spirit used the simple act of dropping a piece of mail off to bump into a lady I hadn't seen in years. Where I normally drop the mail in the outside mailbox, this time I decided to go in.

She had been helping take care of family members in a different state. We were both involved in a mutual ministry at church years ago. We had a delightful time conversing and sharing spiritual conversations, which included recognizing how God orchestrated the little details in both of our lives to meet there.

The Holy Spirit brought a man and me together after months of not running into each other. Funny thing is, we work in the same building but for different companies. When I turned a corner, I saw him at the opposite end. I have continued to pray for his ill son and them as they take such great care of their son at home. Despite the struggles, he continues to smile and have a positive attitude.

We shared our faith and I tried to encourage him with his difficult situation. I hope knowing that others care and are praying for them helps him hold on to his faith.

My faith is strengthened when I see the Holy Spirit at work orchestrating these coincidences, which I consider "God moments" or "God winks." They help me realize how the Spirit is in control. It makes me amazed and in awe of our Creator and seldom surprised because we know He is always at work.

> "The disciples were amazed at his words. But Jesus said again, 'Children, how hard it is to enter the kingdom of God! It is easier for a camel to go through the eye of a needle than for someone who is rich to enter the kingdom of God.' The disciples were even more amazed, and said to each other, 'Who then can be saved?' Jesus looked at them and said, 'With man this is impossible, but not with God; all things are possible with God.'"
> ~ Mark 10:24-27

Isn't it great to see even the disciples, who spent so much time with Jesus, were also amazed at His teachings and the miracles that He performed? They, too, could not figure out how Jesus did these things, yet they were never too surprised to see what He did next.

Be encouraged to…

recognize the Holy Spirit in you.

be amazed, not surprised, when you see the Spirit at work.

reflect on examples of the Lord working things out for you personally.

see the Holy Spirit disguised as coincidences in your life.

share a story with someone of how the Holy Spirit showed up for you.

REFLECTION:

What Holy Spirit arrival did you last experience?
What have you recently put into the hands of the Lord to work out?

"In him we have redemption through his blood, the forgiveness of our trespasses, according to the riches of his grace. In him we have obtained an inheritance, having been predestined according to the purpose of him who works all things according to the counsel of his will, so that we who were the first to hope in Christ might be to the praise of his glory."
~ Ephesians 1:7, 11-12 (ESV)

41

Lighting The Path

One February day, it was a bit cool, crisp, and cloudy when I decided to walk. I saw the sun and blue sky appear and I noticed my shadow directly in front of me. I recalled how, as a child, I was afraid when I saw my own shadow, thinking someone was following me. With this view, I saw a parallel with Jesus representing the sunlight that was shining the path upon all creation.

> *"Jesus once again addressed them: 'I am the world's Light. No one who follows me stumbles around in the darkness. I provide plenty of light to live in.'"*
> ~ John 8:12 (MSG)

Jesus is the light of the world that shines on all of creation. Because of the light, there is no darkness, and we can easily find our way if we follow the path of light. We have the responsibility to continually seek the guiding light, a foretaste of what heaven will be like.

> *"Jesus said, 'For a brief time still, the light is among you. Walk by the light you have so darkness doesn't destroy you. If you walk in darkness, you don't know where you're going. As you have the light, believe in the light. Then the light will be within you, and shining through your lives. You'll be children of light.'"*
> ~ John 12:35-36 (MSG)

Jesus shared these words with the disciples shortly before His death on the cross. He encourages us to walk by the light so we will not be overcome by darkness. When we believe in the light, the light becomes part of us, and we become children of the light. Jesus' light shines through our lives, touching the lives of others.

As I noticed my shadow in front of me, I realized I was walking the illuminated path with Jesus, the light, leading me. What are some verses of encouragement about the path we walk with Jesus?

"Trust in the Lord with all your heart and lean not on
your own understanding; in all your ways submit to
him, and he will make your paths straight."
~ Proverbs 3:5-6

We are encouraged to totally trust the Lord with all our hearts, not trying to reason everything out that happens. It is important that we submit our will and lives to the Lord. He will guide our path.

"You make known to me the path of life; you will fill me with joy
in your presence, with eternal pleasures at your right hand."
~ Psalm 16:11

What joy there is when we experience Jesus' presence with us as we journey this path of life. The joy of the Lord wells up in our spirit, and we can't help but share it with others. The Lord's right hand provides protection and sustainment for us through everything.

"He makes me lie down in green pastures, he leads me beside quiet waters,
he refreshes my soul. He guides me along the right paths for his name's sake."
~ Psalm 23:2-3

As we walk with the Lord, He provides times of refreshment and rest for our sometimes weary spirits. He cares deeply for us and wants the best for His children. His paths for us offer safety and well-being.

It suddenly occurred to me that when I was a child and afraid of my shadow, maybe it was Jesus walking with me, illuminating my path!

Be encouraged to...

> see the light of Jesus guiding your path.
> let Jesus' light in you shine through to others.
> trust the path the Lord is taking you on.
> let joy well up in you as the Lord's right hand sustains you.
> enjoy refreshment while walking in the safety of the Lord.

REFLECTION:

What verse encourages you to know Jesus is always with you?
How do you experience the joy of the Lord?

> *"May God give you more and more grace and peace as you grow in your knowledge of God and Jesus our Lord."*
> ~ 2 Peter 1:2 (NLT)

42

Fire In My Bones

Do you have fire in your bones? The prophet Jeremiah did.

"'Let the prophet who has a dream recount the dream, but let the one who has my word speak it faithfully. For what has straw to do with grain?' declares the Lord. 'Is not my word like fire,' declares the Lord, 'and like a hammer that breaks a rock in pieces?' 'Therefore,' declares the Lord, 'I am against the prophets who steal from one another words supposedly from me.'"
~ Jeremiah 23:28-30

The Lord said His Word is like fire because it goes forth, spreading like wildfire for those who preach it faithfully and sincerely. The Word is timeless and brings salvation to those who accept it. The Lord said His Word is like a hammer as it breaks away our hardness of heart until our hearts beat for Him.

REFLECTION:

When have you experienced God's Word like fire?
When has the Word been like a hammer in your faith journey?

"You deceived me, Lord, and I was deceived; you overpowered me and prevailed. I am ridiculed all day long; everyone mocks me. Whenever I speak, I cry out proclaiming violence and destruction. So the word of the Lord has brought me insult and reproach all day long. But if I say, 'I will not mention his word or speak anymore in his name,' his word is in my heart like a fire, a fire shut up in my bones. I am weary of holding it in; indeed, I cannot."
~ Jeremiah 20:7-9

Christine M. Fisher

When God first called Jeremiah to be a prophet, He told him he would be set over nations and kingdoms but would have to uproot and destroy them and then restore them. Jeremiah did not realize it would be for his own people. Jeremiah found it difficult to share his message of violence and destruction, and naturally, the people were not happy about it. Quite interestingly, despite wanting to stop spreading the bleak message, God's Word was deeply rooted in Jeremiah's heart, and like a fire in his bones, he could not help but share it. He could not contain that fire.

Personally, my writing ministry has been like fire in my bones to share about God's presence and the goodness of His orchestrations. It fills me with joy to have a way to share Him.

REFLECTION:

Does God's Word that is rooted deep in your heart have to be shared? Does the joy of the Lord spill forth from you?

> *"I said, 'I will watch my ways and keep my tongue from sin; I will put a muzzle on my mouth while in the presence of the wicked.' So I remained utterly silent, not even saying anything good. But my anguish increased; my heart grew hot within me. While I meditated, the fire burned; then I spoke with my tongue: 'Show me, Lord, my life's end and the number of my days; let me know how fleeting my life is.'"*
> ~ Psalm 39:1-4

David, who wrote this psalm, tried to remain silent as he feared he would not be able to say anything nice. As he lamented over things that were happening, a fire started burning in his bones that he could not hold in any longer as he pondered God's Word. He had to let the Lord know what was on his heart.

REFLECTION:

What is something you have been struggling with that you have shared with the Lord?

When were you able to silence your tongue instead of hurting someone with your words?

Be encouraged to...

> let God's Word be the fire and hammer in your life.
> release the fire of God's Word from your bones by sharing it with others.
> share with God the struggles or anguish you are experiencing.
> listen more attentively to God's Word.

> *"But when God, who set me apart from my mother's womb*
> *and called me by his grace, was pleased to reveal his Son*
> *in me so that I might preach him among the Gentiles, my*
> *immediate response was not to consult any human being."*
> ~ Galatians 1:15-16

Christine M. Fisher

43

Carry Burdens

I ran into a man who works for a different company in the same building as I work. It had been a few months since I last saw him, and I wondered how his family was doing, as I had been praying for them.

Through a series of orchestrations, I shared one of my books with him eight months earlier. At that time, I was blessed to learn some of his story. He and his wife lovingly provide care for their thirty-year-old son who was born blind and has several health issues that have worsened over the years. Most recently they are trying to control his diabetes, which has unfortunately not improved since I saw him last. I was sad to hear that.

He mentioned he isn't sure God is hearing his prayers, but I was able to say that I see God giving him and his wife the strength day by day to care, with great love, for their son. I hope he felt uplifted knowing that others care and are praying. I pray that he sees God's goodness in providing for them as they faithfully walk this path with their son.

While running an errand a few hours later, my heart was saddened when I overheard a conversation a man was having with another person. He was an older man who had a cane and said at least twice, *"My mom has ruined my life."* This man has been caring for his elderly mom, whose health was declining. He was getting to the point where he could no longer physically care for her, which was a difficult situation. It was disheartening to know he felt his life was ruined so I prayed God would give him strength and help him realize he had been a gift to his mom.

The next day at a church service, I heard a message that was applicable to these situations, which made me reflect on them more.

"Then Jesus said, 'Come to me, all of you who are weary and carry heavy burdens, and I will give you rest. Take my yoke upon you. Let me teach you, because I am humble and gentle at heart, and you will find rest for your souls. For my yoke is easy to bear, and the burden I give you is light.'"
~ Matthew 11:28-30 (NLT)

Jesus' words are so powerful to provide us with encouragement during the difficult times. Have you thought about how Jesus understands the weight of our burdens? He endured the heaviest of burdens, the burden of our sins, and died on the cross for them. In Him, we will find rest as He shares in carrying our burdens.

"So to keep me [Paul] from becoming conceited because of the surpassing greatness of the revelations, a thorn was given me in the flesh, a messenger of Satan to harass me, to keep me from becoming conceited. Three times I pleaded with the Lord about this, that it should leave me. But he said to me, 'My grace is sufficient for you, for my power is made perfect in weakness.' Therefore I will boast all the more gladly of my weaknesses, so that the power of Christ may rest upon me. For the sake of Christ, then, I am content with weaknesses, insults, hardships, persecutions, and calamities. For when I am weak, then I am strong."
~ 2 Corinthians 12:7-10 (ESV)

As Paul had realized in his life, the difficult times, or thorns, as he called them, are opportunities to experience God's grace at work. God's grace is an outpouring of the Holy Spirit. When we are weak and helpless, God is there, giving us the strength and power to carry on as He helps carry our crosses. We are able to be strong because of God's presence and grace. Without God, we would be overwhelmed.

My prayer is that we all realize the truth of these Scriptures during our difficult times. To get through these times, we need love, support, and encouragement from others, along with the grace of God flowing through us.

I will leave you with two interesting thoughts to reflect on...

It is important for us to realize our burdens are lighter because Jesus is with us carrying half of the weight of them.

Jesus had Simon, chosen to help carry His physical cross and God's grace that assisted Him in His most difficult time.

Be encouraged to...

know that Jesus is helping you carry some of your load.
see God's grace assisting you in the difficulties.
accompany others in carrying their crosses.
know when we pray for others, their cross is a little lighter.

REFLECTION:

How did someone else help carry a burden for you?
What burden are you helping to carry for someone?

"And the God of all grace, who called you to his eternal glory
in Christ, after you have suffered a little while, will himself
restore you and make you strong, firm and steadfast."
~ 1 Peter 5:10

44

Coming To Your House

"Jesus entered Jericho and was passing through. A man was there by the name of Zacchaeus; he was a chief tax collector and was wealthy. He wanted to see who Jesus was, but because he was short he could not see over the crowd. So he ran ahead and climbed a sycamore-fig tree to see him, since Jesus was coming that way. When Jesus reached the spot, he looked up and said to him, 'Zacchaeus, come down immediately. I must stay at your house today.' So he came down at once and welcomed him gladly. All the people saw this and began to mutter, 'He has gone to be the guest of a sinner.' But Zacchaeus stood up and said to the Lord, 'Look, Lord! Here and now I give half of my possessions to the poor, and if I have cheated anybody out of anything, I will pay back four times the amount.' Jesus said to him, 'Today salvation has come to this house, because this man, too, is a son of Abraham. For the Son of Man came to seek and to save the lost.'"
~ Luke 19:1-10

Who and what was Zacchaeus like?

He was held in high esteem as the chief tax collector.

He was very wealthy—partly because he told people they owed more than they did.

He had heard about Jesus and was curious to see him.

He was short in stature, so he climbed a sycamore tree to catch a glimpse of Jesus.

He unhesitatingly welcomed Jesus to his house.

He changed the error of his ways because of Jesus' love and being seen by Him.

He had a change of heart willing to share half of his possessions with others.

He wanted to make restitution to those he cheated—giving back four times the amount.

How did Jesus treat Zacchaeus?

While looking up, He took notice of Zacchaeus in the tree.

Jesus knew Zacchaeus had cheated others and still loved him in his sinfulness.

He wanted to get to know Zacchaeus personally.

Jesus sought out Zacchaeus because He wanted him to repent and receive salvation.

In this account, the line that always catches my attention is Jesus saying to Zacchaeus, *"I MUST stay at your house today."*

Take a minute and listen to Jesus say those same words to you personally. *"<Insert your name> I MUST stay at your house today."*

Which of these is your initial response when you hear Jesus say those words?

My house is too messy.

I'm not worthy.

I have to go hide something.

I am too busy.

Yes, Jesus, come and visit.

This is so exciting.

Let me kill the fatted calf.

If your initial response was not like Zacchaeus', may you be encouraged to think about these truths:

Jesus loves you unconditionally—no matter how good or bad you think you are.

> Jesus sees you all the time—you are near and dear to His heart.
> Jesus' arms are always open wide—ready to welcome and embrace you in love.

Jesus is always with you—even though you may feel all alone.

> Jesus cares about the condition of your heart—not the condition of your physical house.
> Jesus knows everything about you—there is nothing about you that He doesn't already know.

Jesus loves and cares for us so much. In fact, He dwells in us! So, He is already at your house. Welcome Him into everything that you do and converse with Him throughout your day. Jesus cares about your worries, anxieties, joys, and sorrows as He continues to reveal Himself to you.

Be encouraged to...

> know Jesus sees you wherever and everywhere you are.
> hear and accept Jesus' invitation calling your name to stay at your house.
> welcome Jesus whole-heartedly into your house and heart even in all of the messes.
> work on changing the error of your ways to be more Christ-like.
> set aside a little, sacred place in your house to commune more intimately with Jesus.

REFLECTION:

Are you ready to welcome Jesus into your house unhesitatingly like Zacchaeus did?
Have you shared deep-seated sorrow, as well as joyful moments, with Jesus?

"Grace and peace to you from God our Father and the Lord Jesus Christ. Praise be to the God and Father of our Lord Jesus Christ, the Father of compassion and the God of all comfort."
~ 2 Corinthians 1:2-3

45

Deafening Silence

Retreats are always a great time to be still with the Lord, as we get away from the busyness of life and the often hectic pace at which we live.

"He says, 'Be still, and know that I am God; I will be exalted among the nations, I will be exalted in the earth.' The Lord Almighty is with us; the God of Jacob is our fortress."
~ Psalm 46:10-11

God tells us, with this passage, to take time to be still, and we will know in our hearts that He is dwelling with us. God and His greatness are exalted among the nations and the entire earth. Yes, the Lord, who is our fortress, is always with us, revealing His presence.

On a retreat weekend, whenever I went outside, I experienced the stillness of all of creation, which brought me a sense of peace and oneness with God. The first night, though, it was not deafening silence. The only sounds I heard were a metal chain banging against the flagpole and two leaves moving along the blacktop. Watching the leaves made me chuckle as one leaf would move and then the other right after the first, making noise as the wind moved them. To me, it was symbolic of the Holy Spirit's wind blowing across the land. Spirit, blow your flame into my spirit.

On the second day, each time I went outside, a deafening silence greeted me, especially at night, while gazing at the many lights along the shoreline and surrounding areas. I soaked in the pure, deafening silence.

Christine M. Fisher

"My heart is not proud, Lord, my eyes are not haughty; I do not concern myself with great matters or things too wonderful for me. But I have calmed and quieted myself, I am like a weaned child with its mother; like a weaned child I am content. Israel, put your hope in the Lord both now and forevermore."
~ Psalm 131:1-3

If we walk humbly with the Lord as our guide, we can move toward a place of calm in our spirit. As we take more time to be still with the Lord, we gain a sense of peace and contentment, just as a nursing baby does. The Lord is our peace and hope.

The stillness of the water, seeing the trees and all of creation, and hearing only the deafening silence filled my spirit with peace and tranquility. Everything was just being as God created it to be. It is a great thing to be one with the Spirit, as we are filled with His presence. The peace we experience indeed goes beyond what our finite minds can understand.

"Don't worry about anything; instead, pray about everything. Tell God what you need, and thank him for all he has done. Then you will experience God's peace, which exceeds anything we can understand. His peace will guard your hearts and minds as you live in Christ Jesus."
~ Philippians 4:6-7 (NLT)

I pray that in the deafening silence, you experience God's presence, where you share your heart's needs and desires with Him. May it yield a peace so beautiful as you live for Jesus each day.

Be encouraged to...

take time each day to be still with the Lord.
recognize the presence of the Lord in the stillness.

experience the peace in the stillness.
put your hope in the Lord.

REFLECTION:

When have you experienced great stillness and God's presence?
When has God's peace flooded your spirit?

"For the Lord God is our sun and our shield. He gives us grace and glory.
The Lord will withhold no good thing from those who do what is right."
~ Psalm 84:11 (NLT)

Christine M. Fisher

46

Sacred Encounters

Easter is the most wonderful time of year because we celebrate the greatest event in all of history—the resurrection of Jesus Christ, which is the central tenet of our faith. We celebrate the victory of the cross and its assurance of eternal life. The different celebrations from Palm Sunday through Easter Sunday are rich and powerful.

I love the sacredness of participating in the foot-washing event like Jesus did with His disciples the night before He died. This year I gained an inner correlation with the outward sign of washing the feet.

The question I reflected on throughout the day was, "What dirt and grime in my soul does God need to wash clean?" My prayer as my feet were being washed was exactly that—"Lord, wash my soul clean. Please make me a new creation, removing the dirt, doubts, and fears. Let me walk confidently with you." It was a beautiful encounter to envision Jesus washing, drying, and kissing both of my feet, then pausing to look into my eyes and smile. At the same time, I know Jesus was cleansing my soul as He heard my heart's cry.

A newer Good Friday tradition for me is to prostrate myself in prayer at the foot of the cross. What a sacred encounter to envision Jesus doing that as He prayed to God, and especially during the hardest moments of His life.

"He took Peter and the two sons of Zebedee along with him, and he began to be sorrowful and troubled. Then he said to them, 'My soul is overwhelmed with sorrow to the point of death. Stay here and keep watch with me.' Going a little farther, he fell with his face to the

ground and prayed, 'My Father, if it is possible, may this cup be taken
from me. Yet not as I will, but as you will.' Then he returned to his
disciples and found them sleeping. 'Couldn't you men keep watch with
me for one hour?' he asked Peter. 'Watch and pray so that you will not
fall into temptation. The spirit is willing, but the flesh is weak.'"
~ Matthew 26:37-41

We have a Savior who understands all of our human emotions because He experienced them in His humanity. After sharing the Last Supper with His disciples, He became sorrowful and troubled, even to the point of death. Jesus took three of the disciples with Him, perhaps because He wanted their support and encouragement to face what was coming next. Jesus needed spiritual family too. Jesus' prayer came from the depth of His being as He prostrated Himself before God, being brutally honest, wondering if there could be a different path for Him to follow. Jesus was disappointed that the disciples fell asleep and told them to be faithful in prayer to not fall into temptation. He knew how often we experience the weakness of the flesh that overtakes us.

I waited patiently for about thirty minutes until everyone finally left before I prostrated myself in prayer in front of the cross. Once again I prayed that I would be a new creation in Him, and tears came to my eyes as I shared my heart with Jesus. Before I left, I inched toward the cross that was in front of me to touch it. I looked to see a puddle of water about the size of an index card. To make sure I was not seeing things, I touched the water. I have no explanation as to where the water came from other than it was a "God moment," as this Scripture came to mind when Jesus was in the Garden of Gethsemane.

"'Father, if you are willing, take this cup from me; yet not my will,
but yours be done.' An angel from heaven appeared to him and
strengthened him. And being in anguish, he prayed more earnestly,
and his sweat was like drops of blood falling to the ground."
~ Luke 22:42-44

Christine M. Fisher

A day after my encounter, I thought about this Scripture that made me appreciate even more the sacredness of the water that was in front of the cross.

"But when they came to Jesus and found that he was already dead,
they did not break his legs. Instead, one of the soldiers pierced Jesus' side
with a spear, bringing a sudden flow of blood and water. The man
who saw it has given testimony, and his testimony is true. He knows
that he tells the truth, and he testifies so that you also may believe."
~ John 19:33-35

God's orchestration led to Jesus' legs not being broken, like was customary. Instead, they lanced Jesus' side, where blood and water started flowing, showing both His humanity and divinity. We have the privilege of having these words and actions written down so we, too, may believe even more.

Be encouraged to...

ask God what cleaning needs to be done in your soul.
prostrate yourself, pouring your heart out to Jesus.
lay your biggest burden down at the foot of the cross.
seek ways to shine your light in the dark parts of this world.

REFLECTION:

What supernatural encounter with God have you experienced?
When was there a time you knew God was changing your heart?

"For the law was given through Moses; grace and
truth came through Jesus Christ."
~ John 1:17

47

New Creations

Is being a Christian like being a pumpkin? It might sound strange but consider how we become a new creation in Christ.

God chooses each of us—you and me—and wants us to be part of His family.

"For he chose us in him before the creation of the world to be holy and blameless in his sight. In love he predestined us for adoption to sonship through Jesus Christ, in accordance with his pleasure and will—to the praise of his glorious grace, which he has freely given us in the One he loves."
- Ephesians 1:4-6

Have you considered how every one of us is God's chosen one? Indeed YOU are His chosen one! We are all God's adopted children because of Jesus' act of salvation. What great love is bestowed upon us.

REFLECTION:

Have you taken time to reflect on and know deep in your heart how you personally are God's chosen one?
What impact does knowing you are God's adopted child have on your life?

God washes away the dirt and cleans us up.

"Now Joshua was dressed in filthy clothes as he stood before the angel. The angel said to those who were standing before him, 'Take off his filthy clothes.' Then he said to Joshua, 'See, I have taken away your sin, and I will put fine garments on you.'"
- Zechariah 3:3-4

Christine M. Fisher

When we come to put our faith and life in Jesus, God washes away the dirt of our past, especially our lack of repentance. God clothed us in the finest of garments when Jesus shed His blood, and we were washed clean. We are new creations.

REFLECTION:

Do you live as a child of God, cleansed by Jesus' blood?
Are you clothed in the fine garments of love and forgiveness?

God softens and opens our hearts as He rids us of all the yucky stuff inside us.

"For I will gather you up from all the nations and bring you home again to your land. Then I will sprinkle clean water on you, and you will be clean. Your filth will be washed away, and you will no longer worship idols. And I will give you a new heart, and I will put a new spirit in you. I will take out your stony, stubborn heart and give you a tender, responsive heart.'"
~ Ezekiel 36:24-26 (NLT)

It takes time for God to rid us of the yucky stuff that is in us as He purifies us daily to become more like Jesus. Sometimes He has to scoop hard to root out of us the sin of pride, envy, or selfishness. Our hearts of stone are replaced with softened hearts and God's spirit of love, peace, and joy.

REFLECTION:

What yucky stuff is God still rooting out of you?
Can you honestly say your heart is more tender and responsive than it is hard?

God carves us a new smiling face as we rejoice in Him.

"Our mouths were filled with laughter, our tongues with songs of joy.
Then it was said among the nations, 'The Lord has done great things for
them.' The Lord has done great things for us, and we are filled with joy."
~ Psalm 126:2-3

As we allow God to work in our lives and hearts, we become the people He intends us to be. We recognize God working in us, and we see the fruits of the Spirit. The fruits of love, joy, peace, forbearance, kindness, goodness, faithfulness, gentleness, and self-control flow from our lives. Our countenances reflect the joy of God's goodness as we rejoice in all He is doing in us.

REFLECTION:

Can people see the joy of the Lord in your face and smile?
What fruit of the Spirit do you need more of?

God puts His light inside us to shine for the entire world to see.

"In the same way, let your light shine before others, that they
may see your good deeds and glorify your Father in heaven."
~ Matthew 5:16

How wonderful it is when we allow God's light to shine in and through our lives into the world. We are transformed people and have the honor and privilege of shining God's light into a sometimes dark world. We shine God's light by doing good as we glorify Him with our lives.

REFLECTION:

What is one way you shine God's light into this world?
Who has lit up your world today by shining God's light?

Be encouraged to reflect on how you are a new creation and...

> you are God's chosen one, adopted into His family.
> you are washed clean by Jesus' blood and clothed in the finest garments.
> God is continually scooping out the yucky stuff and softening your heart.
> God carves a big smile on your face as you rejoice in Him.
> you can shine God's light on all you encounter.

"He generously poured out the Spirit upon us through Jesus Christ
our Savior. Because of his grace he made us right in his sight
and gave us confidence that we will inherit eternal life."
~ Titus 3:6-7 (NLT)

48

Seasonal Names of God

Living in the northeast, I am blessed to experience the seasons to their fullest. I can't help but think how our lives are like the seasons of a tree. I received a card that had a picture of a tree with the leaves divided into four sections with verbiage and leaves appropriate for the season. It said:

LIFE is the spring name of God.
WARMTH is the summer name of God.
COLOR is the autumn name of God.
SILENCE is the winter name of God.

Trees often remind me of God Himself, especially when I see a full-leafed tree standing tall and displaying splendor.

"But blessed are those who trust in the Lord and have made the Lord their hope and confidence. They are like trees planted along a riverbank, with roots that reach deep into the water. Such trees are not bothered by the heat or worried by long months of drought. Their leaves stay green, and they never stop producing fruit."
~ Jeremiah 17:7-8 (NLT)

With our lives rooted in God, we live with trust, hope, and confidence displaying His splendor. Our lives grow in grace as we remain steadfast in the Word of God and prayer even through the difficult trials. The fruitfulness of the Spirit working in us will be evident.

Christine M. Fisher

LIFE IS THE SPRING NAME OF GOD.

"And this is the testimony: God has given us eternal life, and this life is in his Son. Whoever has the Son has life; whoever does not have the Son of God does not have life."
~ 1 John 5:11-12

In the spring, we see nature come to life.

God has given us the greatest gift of life—eternal life—because of His only Son, Jesus, who came to earth for our salvation. Eternal life is life in Jesus, which starts while we are on this earth. Since it is eternal, it also extends all the way to heaven.

LIFE is the spring name of God.
How is God providing new LIFE in you?

WARMTH IS THE SUMMER NAME OF GOD.

"For the Lord God is our sun and our shield. He gives us grace and glory. The Lord will withhold no good thing from those who do what is right."
~ Psalm 84:11 (NLT)

Our sun and our shield are God, who provides the warmth in our lives and protects us. God, being the sun in our lives, represents the glorious source of the light of life that is in us. The sun illuminates our lives with the warmth of His goodness, grace, and glory.

WARMTH is the summer name of God.
How is God producing WARMTH for you?

COLOR IS THE AUTUMN NAME OF GOD.

"You are the light of the world. A town built on a hill cannot be hidden. Neither do people light a lamp and put it under a bowl. Instead they put it on its stand, and it gives light to everyone in the house. In the same way, let your light shine before others, that they may see your good deeds and glorify your Father in heaven."
~ Matthew 5:14-16

In the autumn, we see the greatest display of color.

Made in God's image, we show our colors by shining our light, which brightens the lives of others, by sharing Scripture, having a listening ear, or offering encouragement. Others will encounter God's goodness through our acts of kindness and allow them to glorify God too.

COLOR is the autumn name of God.
How is God displaying COLOR in your current season?

SILENCE IS THE WINTER NAME OF GOD.

"For God alone, O my soul, wait in silence, for my hope is from him."
~ Psalm 62:5 (ESV)

In the winter, silence is most prominent.

During the winter season, we often see no signs of life, especially in nature. The trees are barren and there are no flowers blooming, yet beneath the surface, there is still life going on. We might see nothing, so life seems silent. We still maintain hope, for we know that in the spring, new life will appear.

SILENCE is the winter name of God.
How is God leading you to SILENCE?

Christine M. Fisher

Be encouraged to…

reflect on what attributes of God remind you of trees.
give thanks to God for the gift of eternal life.
bask in the warmth of God's goodness.
display the colors of God's illumination in your faith.
be silent with God knowing He is at work.
reflect on what season is prominent in your life currently.

REFLECTION:

Which season do you have the hardest time relating to?
What deed is God calling you to do to share His color?

*"I will meditate on your majestic, glorious splendor
and your wonderful miracles."*
~ Psalm 145:5 (NLT)

49

Behold

What if we take more time to "behold" all the things God has made? Warning—it requires that we slow down and enjoy what is in front of us, taking time to soak in the beauty.

The Oxford Languages online dictionary defines "behold" as: "to see or observe (a thing or person, especially a remarkable or impressive one)" while a definition from the Merriam-Webster online dictionary is: "to gaze upon."

So if we are to "behold" something, we should observe and gaze upon the impressive things that are in our path.

I never pondered the scriptural significance of the simple word "behold." Researching the word, there are claims that the word "behold" occurs between 1,200 and 1,700 times in Scripture, used mostly in the King James or English Standard versions. Other translations use the word "look" or "see."

Scripturally, "behold" is used to alert us to something significant that we can view with wonder and awe. God has given humanity eyes, ears, and our minds to enjoy the sights and sounds of this magnificent world. It is also a call to action to reflect on God at work and His promises that apply to our lives.

"And God said, 'Behold, I have given you every plant yielding seed that is on the face of all the earth, and every tree with seed in its fruit. You shall have them for food. And to every beast of the earth and to every bird

*of the heavens and to everything that creeps on the earth, everything that
has the breath of life, I have given every green plant for food.' And it was
so. And God saw everything that he had made, and behold, it was very
good. And there was evening and there was morning, the sixth day."*
~ Genesis 1:29-31 (ESV)

In Genesis, where God created the world, we see the word "behold." What
gratitude I have when I reflect on His mighty plan providing food for our
nourishment AND for everything He created. Remember to gaze upon
the beauty of yourself too. You are an impressive creation!

*"Remember not the former things, nor consider the things of old. Behold,
I am doing a new thing; now it springs forth, do you not perceive
it? I will make a way in the wilderness and rivers in the desert."*
~ Isaiah 43:18-19 (ESV)

God is always doing new things in our lives. He sent Jesus to pave the way,
showing us the path that leads to salvation. We are not to get stuck in the
past but know that Jesus leads and guides us forward if we remain open.

*"John [the Baptist] answered them, 'I baptize with water, but among
you stands one you do not know, even he who comes after me, the
strap of whose sandal I am not worthy to untie.' These things took
place in Bethany across the Jordan, where John was baptizing.
The next day he saw Jesus coming toward him, and said, 'Behold,
the Lamb of God, who takes away the sin of the world!'"*
~ John 1:26-29 (ESV)

John the Baptist, Jesus' cousin, was the forerunner of Jesus, baptizing
people with water as they came to believe in Him. John's most important
message for us was that Jesus is the Lamb of God, who would sacrifice
His life for us, taking away our sin. This is one of the most important
proclamations to reflect on and give heartfelt thanks for.

"Behold, I stand at the door and knock. If anyone hears my voice and opens the door, I will come in to him and eat with him, and he with me."
~ Revelation 3:20 (ESV)

Jesus relentlessly pursues us as He knocks at the door of our hearts. When we hear Him calling and open that door, Jesus' loving arms welcome us back. He comes to "feast" with us and give us life in abundance. What a beautiful image of being one with Jesus.

Be encouraged to…

> slow down and gaze upon the impressive beauty in all of creation.
> know that everything God created is worthy to "behold."
> seek with the eyes of your heart the new paths where He is leading you.
> express your gratitude for the Lamb of God who was slain for you.
> open the door of your heart to Jesus and "feast" on life in abundance.

REFLECTION:

Which of the Scriptures are you being called to meditate on?
What do you have gratitude for that God brought to mind?

> *"As God's co-workers we urge you not to receive God's grace in vain. For he says, 'In the time of my favor I heard you, and in the day of salvation I helped you.' I tell you, now is the time of God's favor, now is the day of salvation."*
> ~ 2 Corinthians 6:1-2

50

Care For

A friend and I get together monthly and enjoy a meal, a walk, and spiritual conversations. Once she asked for assistance with two small tasks that needed two people. The next morning as she was praying, the word "care" came to her. She pointed out the difference between when we "care about" someone and when we "care for" someone.

To "care about" someone
is not necessarily
doing anything action-wise—
it is more expressing concern or interest.

To "care for" someone
is to actively engage
and demonstrate your care—
taking action to positively impact,
help, and/or protect another.

My friend experiences the "care for" from both God and me when we gather in fellowship. She feels God's love and care in the simple acts of kindness shared during our visits. It made me reflect on and realize the importance of our need to "care for" others that we encounter daily.

Do we need to pay closer attention to how we "care for" others?
Do we give thanks for how others "care for" us?

What are some Scripture verses that talk about the importance of "care for" others?

"When the Son of Man comes in his glory, and all the angels with him,
he will sit on his glorious throne. All the nations will be gathered before
him, and he will separate the people one from another as a shepherd
separates the sheep from the goats. He will put the sheep on his right and
the goats on his left. Then the King will say to those on his right, 'Come,
you who are blessed by my Father; take your inheritance, the kingdom
prepared for you since the creation of the world. For I was hungry and
you gave me something to eat, I was thirsty and you gave me something
to drink, I was a stranger and you invited me in, I needed clothes and
you clothed me, I was sick and you looked after me, I was in prison and
you came to visit me.' Then the righteous will answer him, 'Lord, when
did we see you hungry and feed you, or thirsty and give you something
to drink? When did we see you a stranger and invite you in, or needing
clothes and clothe you? When did we see you sick or in prison and go to
visit you?' The King will reply, 'Truly I tell you, whatever you did for
one of the least of these brothers and sisters of mine, you did for me.'"
~ Matthew 25:31-40

Jesus gives specific examples of ways we can "care for" others, putting our love and concern into action. We are to "care for" those in need, talk to strangers and possibly invite them for a visit, take care of the sick, and visit the lonely and imprisoned. These are all concrete ways to "care for" others, doing the will of Jesus and sharing His love.

"Now I hope in the Lord Jesus to send Timothy to you soon, that I
also may be cheered when I learn how you are doing. I have nobody
else like him who will genuinely care for your needs. For all the
others look after their own interests, not those of Jesus Christ."
~ Philippians 2:19-21 (BSB)

Paul emphasized to those in Philippi the importance of "caring for" others' needs, as Timothy was modeling. He encourages us to not be so concerned with ourselves or our needs; we need to be like Jesus and be concerned with others. We have the responsibility to provide for those in need.

Do you know that God not only cares about you, but also truly "cares for" you?

> *"Cast all your anxiety on him because he cares for you."*
> ~ 1 Peter 5:7

> *"For I can do everything through Christ, who gives me strength."*
> ~ Philippians 4:13 (NLT)

> *"Peace I leave with you; my peace I give you. I do not give to you as the world gives. Do not let your hearts be troubled and do not be afraid."*
> ~ John 14:27

> *"For he will order his angels to protect you wherever you go."*
> ~ Psalm 91:11 (NLT)

> *"It is the Lord who goes before you. He will be with you; he will not leave you or forsake you. Do not fear or be dismayed."*
> ~ Deuteronomy 31:8 (ESV)

God, our loving Father, goes to great lengths to let us know how special we are to Him. He loves and "cares for" us, even more than our finite minds can comprehend. God lavishes gifts on us, His children—like…

the ability to cast all our anxiety upon Him.
strength so we can do everything through Jesus.
the gift of peace despite the storms that are raging in our lives.
protection wherever we go.
His promise that He is always with us and He will never leave us.

We are so blessed to be the recipients of God's "care for" us.

Be encouraged to…

    be purposeful to "care for" others rather than just care about them.
    share gratitude with the person that showed "care for" you.
    ask God to help you meet a need in someone's life.
    genuinely sacrifice meeting one of your interests to serve someone.
    record for a day the ways you see God "care for" you.

REFLECTION:

How has God shown you that He "cares for" you?
What action item can you do to show someone you "care for" them?

"Do not withhold good from those to whom it is due, when it is in your power to act. The Lord mocks the mockers but is gracious to the humble."
~ Proverbs 3:27, 34

Christine M. Fisher

51

Preparing Us

"God is always preparing us."

This is a simple, yet profound statement voiced by a friend, Lilly. When we live in faith, we know that God is both preparing and orchestrating the events in our lives for our own good and His glory. Often times, we might not see the truth until, in hindsight, we take time to reflect on how things worked out.

God sent John the Baptist to help prepare the way for Jesus' life.

"The beginning of the good news about Jesus the Messiah, the Son of God, as it is written in Isaiah the prophet: 'I will send my messenger ahead of you, who will prepare your way—a voice of one calling in the wilderness, "Prepare the way for the Lord, make straight paths for him."' And so John the Baptist appeared in the wilderness, preaching a baptism of repentance for the forgiveness of sins."
~ Mark 1:1-4

God prepared Jesus' path by having John the Baptist, His cousin, proclaim to the people that the Messiah would be coming. John's life mission was to tell the good news of repentance for their sins and help make their lives right with the coming of Jesus. They were to live in a righteous manner as they awaited the Savior of the world.

God provides us with perfect orchestrations to prepare the way for Him in our lives.

"However, as it is written: What no eye has seen, what no ear has heard, and what no human mind has conceived—the things God has prepared for those who love him—these are the things God has revealed to us by his Spirit. The Spirit searches all things, even the deep things of God."
~ 1 Corinthians 2:9-10

God is continually preparing things for those who love Him. The Spirit knows our true selves, both the seen and unseen. As we grow closer to God, He reveals more things to us through His Spirit.

Forty-five years ago, Lilly and Greg were involved with a ministry called Marriage Encounter, whose aim is to help couples grow closer and deepen their love for each other. Though their children were young, they would travel wherever they were needed. They had a church community that would take turns caring for their children so they could attend the weekends. New York City was one of the places they traveled to as they gave their talks.

A few years later, when Greg started experiencing the beginning of his health issues, they were referred to a hospital in New York City, where he had his surgery. Lilly sees how God prepared them a place to stay with the couples they met while working with Marriage Encounter. They welcomed them with open arms into their homes and they helped in different ways.

In my own life, God prepared the orchestration of publishing numerous books through more than eleven years of writing. Truthfully, it didn't seem like God was doing anything other than allowing me to share with just a few people each week. But God was still working, lining up the orchestrations in my life and in many others. His perfect timing led to more personal growth in me and put the right people in my path to start the first book. The book ministry has led to sharing with more people, and I received the gift of meeting spirit-filled people to help me grow in my faith.

Be encouraged to…

thank God for someone He used to help prepare you for something greater.
reflect on how God is preparing you for something new.
be grateful for the orchestration you see He provided.

REFLECTION:

What was an event you saw God prepare for you?
How did God use you to prepare and provide for someone?

"So God can point to us in all future ages as examples of the
incredible wealth of his grace and kindness toward us, as shown
in all he has done for us who are united with Christ Jesus. For we
are God's masterpiece. He has created us anew in Christ Jesus,
so we can do the good things he planned for us long ago."
~ Ephesians 2:7, 10 (NLT)

52

Weather the Storm

Rain was forecast for three of the four days my husband and I were at Lake Ontario, but God provided a balance of rain, dryness, and sun each day. While observing both the storms and better weather, I thought of how God's inanimate creations of the water, the sky, and the wind go through rough times just as we do.

"But God made the earth by his power; he founded the world by his wisdom and stretched out the heavens by his understanding. When he thunders, the waters in the heavens roar; he makes clouds rise from the ends of the earth. He sends lightning with the rain and brings out the wind from his storehouses."
~ Jeremiah 10:12-13

We know that our all-wise God, in His power, created the heavens, the earth, and everything on the earth, as well as human beings, the greatest of His creations. Not only did He create them, He also controls the waters, the clouds, and the wind. There is no one more powerful or majestic than God.

At the lake, there were a few days and times of intense storming where the sky would be filled with dark clouds, sometimes making it impossible to see the lake right before us. The lake water would become more turbulent, violent, and "angry," as my husband called it. The wind would howl and blow intensely, making the tree branches bend and sway.

After the storm, part of the sky would brighten until eventually the whole sky was a baby blue color with clouds that looked like cotton balls. The

Christine M. Fisher

water would be calm, still, and peaceful, even appearing like a sheet of glass. The wind would die down, and if we were lucky, we would have a gentle breeze to keep us cool.

Do the patterns of the sky, the water, and the wind remind you of when we experience both periods of struggles and then peace?

> *"Some went out on the sea in ships;*
> *they were merchants on the mighty waters.*
> *They saw the works of the Lord,*
> *his wonderful deeds in the deep.*
> *For he spoke and stirred up a tempest*
> *that lifted high the waves.*
> *They mounted up to the heavens and went down to the depths;*
> *in their peril their courage melted away.*
> *They reeled and staggered like drunkards;*
> *they were at their wits' end.*
> *Then they cried out to the Lord in their trouble,*
> *and he brought them out of their distress.*
> *He stilled the storm to a whisper;*
> *the waves of the sea were hushed.*
> *They were glad when it grew calm,*
> *and he guided them to their desired haven.*
> *Let them give thanks to the Lord for his unfailing love*
> *and his wonderful deeds for mankind.*
> *Let them exalt him in the assembly of the people*
> *and praise him in the council of the elders."*
> ~ Psalm 107:23-32

In the storms of life, what three takeaways can we see from this Scripture?

CRY OUT TO THE LORD.

It is important to be honest with the Lord whether we are enjoying blessings or in the messiest parts of our lives. He wants to join in our sufferings and is always there waiting for us to share our hearts with Him as we walk together.

THE LORD WILL BRING US OUT OF OUR DISTRESS.

Isn't it comforting to know that the Lord will bring us out of our distress? He walks with us through our storms, and we know that eventually He will bring us out of them. One way or another, the Lord will find a way to calm the storm.

THE LORD WILL GUIDE US TO SAFETY.

The Lord loves and cares deeply for us. As we grow deeper in faith and trust, we know that He leads us to safety no matter what we are weathering. The Lord assures us in His Word that He is our refuge and will guide us to a safe place.

God is always with us, in both the rough and smooth times. Reflect on this excerpt from an original Spanish prayer entitled Nada Te Turbe (Let Nothing Disturb You).

> *"Let nothing disturb you,*
> *nothing shake you.*
> *Everything passes,*
> *God does not change.*
> *Even if everything is lost,*
> *God alone suffices."*
> ~ St. Teresa of Avila

Christine M. Fisher

Be encouraged to…

let the Lord weather the storms with you.
see the Lord bring you out of your distress.
seek refuge with the Lord.

REFLECTION:

What was one of your lowest points when you cried out to the Lord?
What storm did the Lord bring you through?

"The grace of our Lord Jesus Christ be with your
spirit, brothers and sisters. Amen."
~ Galatians 6:18

53

Greatness

What makes someone great? Is someone great if they...

> have a PhD?
> are a millionaire?
> won an Olympic medal?
> are a brilliant composer?

With all these cases, greatness is measured by what they have accomplished. What if we were to measure true greatness by who we become inwardly?

WE BECOME ADOPTED CHILDREN.

> *"In love he predestined us for adoption to himself as sons through Jesus Christ, according to the purpose of his will, to the praise of his glorious grace, with which he has blessed us in the Beloved."*
> ~ Ephesians 1:5-6 (ESV)

When we come to the point in our lives when we accept Jesus as our personal Savior, the fact that we are God's adopted sons and daughters takes on greater meaning. Jesus is our brother. Our hearts begin to understand how magnificent it is to be called God's beloved. We know that God is leading our lives, and we praise Him for His goodness and grace.

WE BECOME LOVE ITSELF—AS WE LOVE GOD AND OTHERS.

"If anyone acknowledges that Jesus is the Son of God, God lives in them
and they in God. And so we know and rely on the love God has for us.
God is love. Whoever lives in love lives in God, and God in them."
~ 1 John 4:15-16

"Jesus replied: 'Love the Lord your God with all your heart and with
all your soul and with all your mind.' This is the first and greatest
commandment. And the second is like it: 'Love your neighbor as yourself.'"
~ Matthew 22:37-39

"God is love"—three simple words that are so powerful. If we believe in
God that means His love is in us. We are blessed to love God with all of our
being and to love ourselves and others with that same love. It is a life-long
process of growing deeper in becoming love and sharing it with others.

WE BECOME SAINTS—LIVING HOLY AND BLAMELESSLY.

"Paul, an apostle of Christ Jesus by the will of God, To the saints who
are in Ephesus, and are faithful in Christ Jesus: Grace to you and peace
from God our Father and the Lord Jesus Christ. Blessed be the God and
Father of our Lord Jesus Christ, who has blessed us in Christ with every
spiritual blessing in the heavenly places, even as he chose us in him before the
foundation of the world, that we should be holy and blameless before him."
~ Ephesians 1:1-4 (ESV)

Have you considered yourself a saint? Easton's Bible Dictionary defines a
"saint" as: "one separated from the world and consecrated to God; a be-
liever in Christ." God has called you to be a saint, one who is consecrated
to God and believes in Christ. You can be holy and blameless despite being
a sinner. Saints are not perfect but have a desire to please the Lord.

We are all on a journey to our heavenly home to spend eternity in the true presence of God and Jesus. We become the people God intends us to be through the ways we grow in knowing we are God's beloved child, experience and share His great love, and become saints living holy and blameless lives. Our vocations and accomplishments help us to grow closer to God and to glorify Him. Our accomplishments should help us spread God's goodness and peace to all. We strive, with God's help, to become more Christ-like each day of our lives.

Be encouraged to...

> reflect on the fact you are God's adopted child.
> grow deeper in loving God, others, and yourself.
> thank God that you are a saint who is trying your best.

REFLECTION:

Who do you need to love more—God, others, or yourself?
What is one unique way you reflect God's greatness?

> *"Therefore, preparing your minds for action, and being*
> *sober-minded, set your hope fully on the grace that will be*
> *brought to you at the revelation of Jesus Christ."*
> ~ 1 Peter 1:13 (ESV)

54

The Sparrows

Have you ever felt small and insignificant?

Like you were all alone, though you know the truth of God's Word that He is always with you, leading and guiding?

Don't we sometimes let our feelings triumph over the reality we might need to be reminded of?

One year when I was traveling to the Christian Literary Awards in Arlington, Texas, I felt small and insignificant while walking amid a sea of people at the airports. Two of the three airports were massive, and there were crowds everywhere.

It was a little less crowded at the baggage claim, where I waited for my bag. As I stepped away to find the hotel shuttle area, God sent me a heart reminder that was in a tile on the floor. I smiled, remembering how much He loves me and how I am to share that love with others.

When I walked outside to wait for the hotel shuttle, there were a few people around. I happened to sit on a ledge where I observed three sparrows, reminding me of the Trinity. Immediately, I felt it was God's message to me that "His eye is on me," just as His eye is on the sparrows. God was with me as I recalled a passage about the sparrows.

"You can buy two sparrows for only a copper coin, yet not even one sparrow falls from its nest without the knowledge of your Father. Aren't you worth much more to God than many sparrows? So don't worry. For your Father cares deeply about even the smallest detail of your life."
~ Matthew 10:29-31 (TPT)

Sparrows are one of the smallest of birds that are mentioned a few times in the Bible, symbolizing something of minimal value. From this passage, we see that a single copper coin, worth little, was enough for two sparrows. Often, the sparrows would be food for the poor. Since God cares even for the insignificant, small sparrows, we know He cares even more for each one of us made in His image. How comforting to know in our hearts that God cares about even the littlest detail in our lives.

"God of Heaven's Armies, you find so much beauty in your people! They're like lovely sanctuaries of your presence. Deep within me are these lovesick longings, desires and daydreams of living in union with you. When I'm near you, my heart and my soul will sing and worship with my joyful songs of you, my true source and spring of life! O Lord of Heaven's Armies, my King and my God, even the sparrows and swallows are welcome to build a nest among your altars to raise their young. What pleasure fills those who live every day in your temple, enjoying you as they worship in your presence! How enriched are they who find their strength in the Lord; within their hearts are the highways of holiness!"
~ Psalm 84:1-5 (TPT)

Once again, we learn how seemingly insignificant and small sparrows are yet important and valuable to God. He made the sparrows, so they have unlimited access to build nests for their young among the altars, the place where Israel first had access to communion with God. The sparrows commune with God too. How many more privileges do we, as humans, have where we can worship and praise God continually? There is joy and strength when we take time to worship the Creator.

As only God can do, the next morning a friend on social media posted a lyric to the song "His Eye is on the Sparrow." I smiled at the lyric,

His eye is on the sparrow,
And I know he watches me.

Christine M. Fisher

When you hear the birds singing praises to God, may it be a reminder to you that you are cared for and important in God's eyes.

Be encouraged to remember the sparrows and know that...

> God's eye is on you.
> you are even more valuable than they are.
> God cares about the littlest details in your life.
> you, too, are invited to God's altar.
> you live in God's presence continually.
> it is a great privilege to worship God.

REFLECTION:

What lesson from the sparrows speaks most to your heart?
How has God let you know recently that He values and sees you?

> *"For from his fullness we have all received, grace upon grace."*
> ~ John 1:16 (ESV)

55

High-Five

When is the last time you gave yourself a high-five? At a retreat, I was encouraged to stand in front of the mirror and high-five myself. When I tried it, I smiled, which surprised me.

Maybe, like me, you have only given a high-five to other people. What are some reasons we high-five?

Maybe to...

> celebrate a great accomplishment.
> give positive reinforcement.
> build team or individual spirit.
> show someone they are seen and valued.

It is quite simple and might be beneficial to give yourself a high-five each day. It gives us a chance to look in the mirror and see not only God's reflection but also to celebrate the goodness of God in us. It is an opportunity to love ourselves as God does, which is usually harder for us. Look into your eyes that lead to the beauty of your heart and soul. God is our biggest cheerleader since He created us in love. What did Jesus tell us?

"Jesus replied: 'Love the Lord your God with all your heart and with all your soul and with all your mind. This is the first and greatest commandment. And the second is like it: Love your neighbor as yourself.'"
~ Matthew 22:37-39

Christine M. Fisher

Jesus shared how the most important thing we can do is to love God with all of our hearts, soul, and mind—the totality of us. Then we need to love equally ourselves and everyone that God created. Doesn't it make sense that the degree that we love ourselves is the degree to which we love others? The love we have for ourselves is foundational to our relationship with others. As we grow in loving ourselves, we will find that our relationships and love for others will grow too.

What are some reasons to celebrate ourselves in the mirror daily with a high-five, even multiple times?

WE ARE CREATED IN THE IMAGE AND LIKENESS OF GOD.

"Then God said, 'Let us make mankind in our image, in our likeness, so that they may rule over the fish in the sea and the birds in the sky, over the livestock and all the wild animals, and over all the creatures that move along the ground.' So God created mankind in his own image, in the image of God he created them; male and female he created them. God saw all that he had made, and it was very good. And there was evening, and there was morning—the sixth day."
~ Genesis 1:26-27, 31

One of our greatest blessings is that we are made in God's image and likeness. No other creation can say that. Notice how this day of creation says, *"It was very good,"* while the other days say *"good."* What a gift it is to know we reflect and express the image of God.

WE ARE WONDERFULLY MADE BY GOD.

"For you created my inmost being; you knit me together in my mother's womb. I praise you because I am fearfully and wonderfully made; your works are wonderful, I know that full well."
~ Psalm 139:13-14

God knit everyone together, including you and me, in our mother's womb. We were created on purpose for His purpose. He made each of us unique and wonderful for the glory of His name. Everything God makes, does, and orchestrates is beautiful, too. He is the Creator of all.

WE CAN DO AMAZING THINGS WITH GOD.

> *"God can do anything, you know—far more than you could ever imagine or guess or request in your wildest dreams! He does it not by pushing us around but by working within us, his Spirit deeply and gently within us. Glory to God in the church! Glory to God in the Messiah, in Jesus! Glory down all the generations! Glory through all millennia! Oh, yes!"*
> ~ Ephesians 3:20-21 (MSG)

God is so awesome that He gave us the Holy Spirit that guides us daily. He is often the still, small voice that helps direct our paths and actions. He nudges gently and guides our lives as we try to glorify God with all we do in His name. We are only able to do these things because of the Spirit's power—we can do nothing on our own.

WE ARE SEEN AND VALUED BY GOD.

> *"For the eyes of the Lord run to and fro throughout the whole earth, to give strong support to those whose heart is blameless toward him..."*
> ~ 2 Chronicles 16:9 (ESV)

> *"Are not two sparrows sold for a penny? Yet not one of them will fall to the ground outside your Father's care. And even the very hairs of your head are all numbered. So don't be afraid; you are worth more than many sparrows."*
> ~ Matthew 10:29-31

God always sees us because He is omnipresent, always being everywhere. We are important to Him because He created us in love and loves us

Christine M. Fisher

unconditionally. He wants us to have hearts full of love as we strive to live blameless and righteous lives. God values and cares for us even more than He does the sparrows, which are always under His protection.

May you delight in these quotes when you are looking in the mirror and giving yourself a high-five—rejoicing in your beauty just like God does.

"Remarkably, the Lord made you in His very own image. That means your life is sacred. It has value. You have been made by love and with love. It is hard to believe, but you look a lot like God."
~ Allen Hunt

"Be yourself; everybody else is taken."
~ Oscar Wilde

Be encouraged to…

look in the mirror at least once a day and give yourself a high-five.
work on loving yourself as much as you love others.
reflect on how you are made in God's image and likeness.
thank God for being wonderfully and fearfully made.
ask God what amazing things you can do with Him.
live in delight knowing you are seen and valued by God.

REFLECTION:

Do you need God's help to love yourself as much as you love your neighbor? What is something amazing God has helped you accomplish?

"I myself am convinced, my brothers and sisters, that you yourselves are full of goodness, filled with knowledge and competent to instruct one another. Yet I have written you quite boldly on some points to remind you of them again, because of the grace God gave me."
~ Romans 15:14-15

Section 3

GOD'S GRACE MANIFESTED THROUGH PEOPLE

"For the Lord God is our sun and our shield. He gives us grace and glory.
The Lord will withhold no good thing from those who do what is right."
~ Psalm 84:11 (NLT)

What a generous God we have! He is the best Father, always looking out for our best interest. He provides the sunlight even during our difficult times. He is our protector and provides us with goodness as we strive to follow His ways. In both the good and bad, we have God's grace and glory accompanying us.

God's grace is experienced first in our lives and transforms us to be more Christ-like. As we grow in His grace, we have the responsibility to share it with all.

God's grace manifested through people.

"I do not at all understand the mystery of grace—only that it meets
us where we are but does not leave us where it found us."
~ Anne Lamont

56

A Time of Grace

Can you think of a time when, despite a rough, stressful season, you saw God working and helping you through? Did you view it as a time of grace?

Times when loved ones are in the hospital and there are more questions than answers are tough. It is an opportunity to pray for the person individually and to ask others to join in prayer.

One year my father-in-law was in the hospital for thirty-two days followed by seven days in rehabilitation. He had two abdominal surgeries within nine days. The doctors were unable to see things well enough to do anything during the second surgery. It was devastating to think they were not able to help him further.

My in-laws have seven kids of which three are local. The families get along well and support each other, especially in being available for their parents to aid them in whatever way they can.

This time of grace seemed magnified because I was able to share it with a friend. It was one of those "God-incidents." The same time my father-in-law was in the hospital, I learned that a friend's mother was in the same hospital. A little prompting had me visit her mom's room. Quite the opposite from our situation that had lots of local people to support them, this friend was the only one there, as her sister lives out of town. That compelled me to visit my friend frequently when I was at the hospital.

"Share each other's burdens, and in this way obey the law of Christ."
~ Galatians 6:2 (NLT)

"Rejoice with those who rejoice; mourn with those who mourn."
~ Romans 12:15

As followers of Christ, we are instructed to share the burdens of those who are heavy-laden. It might be listening to someone, providing food, or physically helping. We journey together with others so we can rejoice and mourn with them.

I was blessed to be able to listen to my friend and share in her journey. It was a special bond that strengthened our friendship. It was also a joy to meet her mother who was a special lady. Every time I would visit, she too, would ask how my father-in-law was progressing. Despite her condition, she cared about someone she never met.

When my friend's mother went to a nursing home, it was hard to see her mom's health decline. She died shortly thereafter. My life was enriched and graced through knowing her. Meeting my friend's sister seemed like we had known each other forever. It was my privilege to attend the funeral for this family and show my love and support for what they were going through.

I am thankful for this time of grace to share the hard struggles of people suffering. Trying to support one another and help in whatever small ways are blessings in our lives, and God always provides what we need.

REFLECTION:

When have you experienced a period of grace?
Who did God put in your path to journey with you in grace?

"Let us approach the throne of grace with confidence, so that we may receive mercy and find grace to help us in our time of need."
~ Hebrews 4:16

Christine M. Fisher

57

God's Always Got You

Think of the times when you prayed for others, even when not asked.

Were you able to pray in person with them?

Did you send them messages of encouragement every now and then?

How constant were you with your prayers?

Have you reached out to ask someone or a group of people for prayer?

Was it through a Facebook group, a church, a website, or a friend?

Did anyone take the time to pray with you right then and there?

Did you get reminders every now and then that you were being prayed for?

Could you feel in your spirit the power of these prayers?

When I recently asked for prayer in a Christian community via an email, my spirit was encouraged when I read...

"I got you!
We got you!"

The few words spoke volumes and filled my spirit with joy. A smile came to my face as I let the words settle into my soul. While reading those words, knowing that prayer warriors were praying with heartfelt sincerity brought me...

comfort

hope

encouragement

peace.

"Praise be to the God and Father of our Lord Jesus Christ, the
Father of compassion and the God of all comfort, who comforts
us in all our troubles, so that we can comfort those in any
trouble with the comfort we ourselves receive from God."
~ 2 Corinthians 1:3-4

God is the Father of compassion, which brings us comfort. Consider how God's compassion flows through Jesus and then through us. It is like a never-ending gift that we are honored to experience and share.

"Do not be anxious about anything, but in every situation, by
prayer and petition, with thanksgiving, present your requests to
God. And the peace of God, which transcends all understanding,
will guard your hearts and your minds in Christ Jesus."
~ Philippians 4:6-7

As we pray, whether it be praising, petitioning, or thanksgiving, we can experience God's peace, which also gives us hope. We come to encounter God in our prayer along with a peace that the world cannot understand.

I was encouraged more when the person would mention the prayer requests in a text along with those words...

"I got you!
We got you!"

I knew how committed they were to prayer, and it brought me continued comfort and peace. I felt the sincerity of the people being...

concerned

caring

genuine

loving.

"Carry each other's burdens, and in this way
you will fulfill the law of Christ."
~ Galatians 6:2

By walking with people through difficult times, we show our love for one another, which fulfills the two great commandments Jesus gave. We are to love God above all and our neighbor as ourselves.

"Therefore if you have any encouragement from being united with Christ,
if any comfort from his love, if any common sharing in the Spirit, if any
tenderness and compassion, then make my joy complete by being like-
minded, having the same love, being one in spirit and of one mind."
~ Philippians 2:1-2

Being united with Christ, we have the privilege of sharing love, tenderness, compassion, and joy with everyone. We are one in spirit with Christ, which we can share with others.

Another friend lived this sincerity of prayer by stopping at a sacred place to pray for my intentions, sending me a picture, and wishing me a peace-filled day. It was a gesture that touched my heart, knowing someone cared and felt inspired to go the extra mile. As the words...

"I got you!
We got you!"

echoed in my mind, I couldn't help but think that God was also speaking those words to me and you.

Yes,

"God's always
got us!"

"Don't be afraid, for I am with you. Don't be discouraged,
for I am your God. I will strengthen you and help you. I
will hold you up with my victorious right hand."
~ Isaiah 41:10 (NLT)

God is God, who is above all. Therefore, we do not need to be afraid or discouraged. God promises to strengthen and help us. We have the victory with God's right hand. God's always got us!

"I can never escape from your Spirit! I can never get
away from your presence! If I go up to heaven, you are
there; if I go down to the grave, you are there."
~ Psalm 139:7-8 (NLT)

We cannot get away from God no matter where we go. God is everywhere, from heaven to the grave. What a comfort to know that He is always with us.

Be encouraged to...

share the phrase *"I got you"* with sincerity to someone in need.
let someone know you are faithfully praying for them through their difficulties.
reach out to a trusted person if you need some prayer.
remember that God's always got us!

REFLECTION:

What trial did you know without a doubt that God had you?
Who have you walked with letting them know you and God had them?

> *"And God raised us up with Christ and seated us with him*
> *in the heavenly realms in Christ Jesus, in order that in the*
> *coming ages he might show the incomparable riches of his*
> *grace, expressed in his kindness to us in Christ Jesus."*
> ~ Ephesians 2:6-7

58

The Mighty Oak Tree

On my birthday, I received a unique gift: a handcrafted wooded acorn. It included a note that is applicable to our lives and worthy of reflection.

"Looking at an acorn, it's hard to tell that it will one day be a great oak tree. Similarly, when we look at our lives, we seldom know what the future will hold. God not only sees where you are right now but also who you will become and where you will go. He doesn't see an acorn; He sees a mighty oak tree! He knows the plans He has for you and what He wants to do through you. Keep stretching, growing, and challenging yourself, and trust that God is using your gifts to make a difference in this world. You are amazing, and we are grateful to have you in our lives."

What are four takeaways from these words of wisdom?

GOD WANTS US TO GROW SPIRITUALLY FROM AN ACORN TO A MIGHTY OAK TREE.

There is an old proverb: *"Great oaks from little acorns grow."* The old proverb is a powerful parallel to our spiritual journeys. At the point when we accept Jesus as our Lord and Savior, we are like an acorn, a seemingly small creation. As we grow, study the Word, and experience the presence of the Spirit in our lives, we grow into a big oak tree that has strong roots. We grow in love and share that with all.

"To all who mourn in Israel, he will give a crown of beauty
for ashes, a joyous blessing instead of mourning, festive praise

Christine M. Fisher

instead of despair. In their righteousness, they will be like
great oaks that the Lord has planted for his own glory."
~ Isaiah 61:3 (NLT)

Indeed, we are planted to bring glory to the Lord in all that we do and are. As we strive to live righteously and victoriously, we emulate more of God's glory.

We may experience times of growth spurts and also times of what feels like no growth. Sometimes we might not see the growth, but others who walk with us might. Life is full of choices. Some things we have control over and some we do not. God knows the master plan of our lives and sees the beauty of the mighty oak tree of our lives if we remain faithful to Him. He is our biggest cheerleader, believing in us and seeing the best in us.

GOD HAS PLANS FOR EACH OF US TO SPREAD THE GOOD NEWS OF JESUS.

"For I know the plans I have for you," says the Lord. "They are plans
for good and not for disaster, to give you a future and a hope."
~ Jeremiah 29:11 (NLT)

"Preach the word of God. Be prepared, whether the time is favorable or not.
Patiently correct, rebuke, and encourage your people with good teaching."
~ 2 Timothy 4:2 (NLT)

From the beginning of time, God only wanted the best for us, His children. He wants us to live in His goodness and with hope in Him. God continually lavishes His unconditional love on us. He gave us free will to choose Him and to walk humbly with Him each day. Our lives are an offering to God.

God wants to work through us in the unique way that He provides. We share in preaching the good news of Jesus, some as teachers, preachers, musicians, writers, and some as ordinary people helping a stranger, feeding the hungry, or visiting a shut-in.

GOD WANTS TO HELP US GROW CONTINUALLY AS WE TRUST HIM WITH OUR GIFTS AND LIVES.

"Now there are varieties of gifts, but the same Spirit; and there are varieties of service, but the same Lord; and there are varieties of activities, but it is the same God who empowers them all in everyone. To each is given the manifestation of the Spirit for the common good."
~ 1 Corinthians 12:4-7 (ESV)

The mighty oak tree is always growing, soaking up the water, extending its roots, and serving a God-ordained purpose. Our lives are just like that mighty oak tree. We need to continually grow in sharing the special gifts God has given us for the good of others. The Spirit flows through the gifts we share. Our gifts can be shared through different official ministries we are a part of or even in our daily dealings with people. God might provide new gifts in our lives as we keep going deeper with Him so that our lives can touch different sets of people. The Spirit is always at work.

GOD WANTS US TO KNOW CHRIST LIVES IN US AND TO HAVE GRATITUDE FOR HOW PEOPLE BLESS OUR LIVES.

"Examine yourselves to see whether you are in the faith; test yourselves. Do you not realize that Christ Jesus is in you—unless, of course, you fail the test?"
~ 2 Corinthians 13:5

"How can we thank God enough for you in return for all the joy we have in the presence of our God because of you?"
~ 1 Thessalonians 3:9

Do you live knowing Christ is in you, shining His light into the lives of others? God loves us so much that He gives us that special gift. We need to believe that goodness is in us because of Christ living in us. We also should be filled with gratitude for the people God brings into our lives to share this journey of faith with.

Be encouraged to…

> reflect on how your life has gone from an acorn to a mighty oak tree.
> continually be seeking God's plan for your life.
> know your gifts are needed to further the kingdom.
> know others appreciate the gift you are.

REFLECTION:

How has God stretched you to share Him?
What is one way God has worked through you?

"… In the same way, the gospel is bearing fruit and growing throughout the whole world—just as it has been doing among you since the day you heard it and truly understood God's grace."
~ Colossians 1:6

59

Let Me Love You

A friend shared how she is learning to accept and receive God's love, something she hadn't experienced before.

> *"Everywhere the Holy One is shouting and whispering,*
> *'Let me love you!'*
> *And all we have to do is receive.*
> *In reality, that is our life's work.*
> *Nothing more and certainly nothing less."*
> ~ Judy Cannato

HEAR GOD SAY TO YOU, *"LET ME LOVE YOU!"*

> *"And so we know and rely on the love God has for us. God is love. Whoever lives in love lives in God, and God in them."*
> ~ 1 John 4:16

Let the three short, powerful words, *"God is love,"* sink into your heart. God is love! We can only love because God is love. We cannot earn God's love. Because God is love, His love is freely available to us. When we experience God's love, we know we live in Him and He lives in us. We are love, too!

> *"You alone are the Lord. You made the skies and the heavens and all the stars. You made the earth and the seas and everything in them. You preserve them all, and the angels of heaven worship you."*
> ~ Nehemiah 9:6 (NLT)

Christine M. Fisher

Consider how God created everything from the beginning of time. He created the light, the skies, waters, land, plants, animals, and you and me. God's love is found in everything He created right from the start. God created everything in order to give Himself away in love.

"And the Lord God made clothing from animal
skins for Adam and his wife."
~ Genesis 3:21 (NLT)

Even after Adam and Eve wanted to become like God and ate from the tree of knowledge, God demonstrated great love for them by providing animal skins for their clothing instead of the fig leaves they sewed. He did not punish them in His wrath, rather, because of God's great love, He provided for them.

ACCEPT AND RECEIVE GOD'S LOVE.

Why do we often struggle with accepting and receiving God's love?

Maybe because we cannot physically see God?
> Instead we can focus on the ways we experience God's presence in our lives.

Maybe because we are focused on the worldly, human way of loving?
> Instead we can experience the unconditional power of divine love.

Maybe because we feel we are unworthy?
> Instead we are reminded we are God's children, made in His image.

Maybe because we are too busy doing things?
> Instead we can take time to just be still with God.

Maybe because we think we have to be in control of our lives?
> Instead we need to be reminded that God is sovereign.

WHAT ARE WAYS WE CAN RECEIVE GOD'S LOVE AND HEAR HIM SAY, *"LET ME LOVE YOU?"*

Reading Scripture to deepen and strengthen our relationship with God.

Being in awe of the beauty of all God's creations.

Thanking God for orchestrating the events in our lives.

Being open to see what signs of love God has in store for us.

Having a heart of gratitude for the people God places in our paths who challenge us to go deeper in our relationship with Him.

Spending time in solitude with Him without using words.

Paying attention and listening to the still, small voice guiding our paths.

Praising God and seeing goodness in everyone, knowing they are His children too.

When we receive God's love, our hearts are open to seeing more of how God is working. The fruits of the Spirit of love, joy, peace, patience, kindness, generosity, faithfulness, gentleness, and self-control shine through our lives. We are better able to love others with God's agape love.

Be encouraged to…

see the ways God is trying to say, *"Let me love you."*

be a receiver of God's love, which is our life's work.

share God's love that you receive with others.

know God is in control.

REFLECTION:

How are you reminded of God's love for you?
Do you find it easy to accept God's love?

> *"May the grace of the Lord Jesus Christ, and the love of God,*
> *and the fellowship of the Holy Spirit be with you all."*
> ~ 2 Corinthians 13:14

60

The Lowly

One Christmas season, the theme of how God chooses the lowly resonated with me. Everyone involved in the events of Jesus' birth and ministry beginnings was considered lowly in the worldly view.

MARY, THE MOTHER OF JESUS

> *"In the sixth month of Elizabeth's pregnancy, God sent the angel*
> *Gabriel to Nazareth, a town in Galilee, to a virgin pledged to*
> *be married to a man named Joseph, a descendant of David.*
> *The virgin's name was Mary. The angel went to her and said,*
> *'Greetings, you who are highly favored! The Lord is with you.'"*
> ~ Luke 1:26-28

Mary, a young girl living a chaste life, had no worldly status, fame, or notoriety, yet God chose her to be highly favored. She was empowered by the Holy Spirit to conceive and carry Jesus, the Savior of the world. Mary, a lowly woman, said yes to God, not knowing what the future held.

JOSEPH, JESUS' EARTHLY FATHER

> *"This is how the birth of Jesus the Messiah came about: His mother*
> *Mary was pledged to be married to Joseph, but before they came*
> *together, she was found to be pregnant through the Holy Spirit. Because*
> *Joseph her husband was faithful to the law, and yet did not want to*
> *expose her to public disgrace, he had in mind to divorce her quietly.*
> *But after he had considered this, an angel of the Lord appeared to*
> *him in a dream and said, 'Joseph son of David, do not be afraid to*

take Mary home as your wife, because what is conceived in her is from
the Holy Spirit. She will give birth to a son, and you are to give him
the name Jesus, because he will save his people from their sins.'"
~ Matthew 1:18-21

Scripture doesn't tell us much about Joseph, and he is not quoted in Scripture. We know he was a carpenter by trade, someone who was not highly esteemed. Joseph was a righteous and caring man, as he did not want to publicly disgrace Mary if he divorced her. He, too, listened to the angel and said yes, taking on the responsibility to be Jesus' earthly father.

JOHN THE BAPTIST, THE FORERUNNER OF JESUS

"And the child (John the Baptist) grew and became strong in spirit, and
he was in the wilderness until the day of his public appearance to Israel."
~ Luke 1:80 (ESV)

"In those days John the Baptist came preaching in the wilderness of Judea,
'Repent, for the kingdom of heaven is at hand.' For this is he who was
spoken of by the prophet Isaiah when he said, 'The voice of one crying in
the wilderness: "Prepare the way of the Lord; make his paths straight."'
Now John wore a garment of camel's hair and a leather belt around his
waist, and his food was locusts and wild honey. Then Jerusalem and all
Judea and all the region about the Jordan were going out to him, and
they were baptized by him in the river Jordan, confessing their sins."
~ Matthew 3:1-6 (ESV)

John the Baptist was the miracle son of Zechariah and Elizabeth. We know John grew up in the Judean Desert and was called by God to preach repentance when he was thirty years old. John was not royalty, but rather lowly by the world's standards. His clothing was made from camel's hair, and he ate locusts and honey while living in the desert.

"And there were shepherds living out in the fields nearby, keeping watch over their flocks at night. An angel of the Lord appeared to them, and the glory of the Lord shone around them, and they were terrified. But the angel said to them, 'Do not be afraid. I bring you good news that will cause great joy for all the people. Today in the town of David a Savior has been born to you; he is the Messiah, the Lord. This will be a sign to you: You will find a baby wrapped in cloths and lying in a manger.'"
~ Luke 2:8-12

Isn't it fascinating to see how God's plan was for the lowly shepherds to be some of the first ones to find out about the birth of Jesus? Just ordinary, simple people tending their flocks were God's chosen ones to announce the good news.

JESUS

"And Joseph also went up from Galilee, from the town of Nazareth, to Judea, to the city of David, which is called Bethlehem, because he was of the house and lineage of David, to be registered with Mary, his betrothed, who was with child. And while they were there, the time came for her to give birth. And she gave birth to her firstborn son and wrapped him in swaddling cloths and laid him in a manger, because there was no place for them in the inn."
~ Luke 2:4-7 (ESV)

Are you in awe considering the lowly, humble manner in which the Savior came to earth? With so many people arriving in Bethlehem to register for the census, they could not find any place to stay as the time came for His birth. Jesus was born in a stable, and His manger was a feeding trough for the animals.

Be encouraged knowing that God uses every one of us, including the lowly, if…

we are open to saying yes to God.

our actions follow God's will.

we let God lead us.

we announce the good news to the world.

we remember that God is with us in every circumstance.

REFLECTION:

Which of the lowly people do you relate to most?

What is something great you have done with God's help?

"Grace and peace to you from God our Father and the Lord Jesus Christ. God chose the lowly things of this world and the despised things—and the things that are not—to nullify the things that are, so that no one may boast before him."
~ 1 Corinthians 1:3, 28-29

61

God's Goodness

"And so we know and rely on the love God has for us. God is love. Whoever lives in love lives in God, and God in them."
~ 1 John 4:16

Did you catch that powerful three-word sentence? *"God is love!"* He is love itself. One of our purposes in life is to become more like God—to be love—to others and to ourselves. We continue to grow in love as we continue to trust God as He takes us into deeper waters in our faith journey.

We are made for love,
      by love [God],
           to be love.

Not only is God love, God is good. It is a double blessing when we experience the true love of God and continually live in His goodness.

"You [God] are good, and what you do is good; teach me your decrees."
~ Psalm 119:68

God's character is *"You are good"* and He lives that goodness out with *"What you do is good."* God lives out what He is: total goodness.

"Give thanks to the Lord, for he is good! His faithful love endures forever."
~ Psalm 107:1 (NLT)

God is everlasting love and goodness. We have so much to give thanks for.

Christine M. Fisher

"Great is the Lord and most worthy of praise; his greatness no one can fathom. One generation commends your works to another; they tell of your mighty acts. They speak of the glorious splendor of your majesty—and I will meditate on your wonderful works. They tell of the power of your awesome works—and I will proclaim your great deeds. They celebrate your abundant goodness and joyfully sing of your righteousness."
~ Psalm 145:3-7

These verses tell of the great and glorious splendor of God's majesty that is all around us and the awesome works and deeds He is doing in our lives. All of it is because of the abundant goodness of God; we need to continually share this with others and sing of His righteous ways.

Relationships are one of the greatest ways we can share God's love and goodness in our lives. The presence of God in us impacts and influences others whenever we reach out and interact with them.

I met a man ten years ago when my youngest son played baseball with his grandson. We have kept in touch with each other through an occasional text or email, and he is always happy to receive one of my books.

We met again in person at a local college baseball game and enjoyed catching up with one another. Because the game was impacted by the weather, we went to dinner and talked about how wonderful it is when one of us reaches out to the other, making us feel valued. We viewed our time together as God's goodness.

That same day, I stopped at a store to buy a gift for a friend who was involved with my latest book. Surprisingly, I met up with him and his wife, who live out of state, the next day and I was able to present the gift and a copy of my book to him. It was a great time of fellowship and a blessing to me. God's love and goodness orchestrated even that little detail in my life.

Be encouraged to…

reflect on how God is love.
take baby steps toward being more like God: to be love.
experience God's character trait of goodness in your life.
focus on being thankful for God's love and goodness.
celebrate God's abundant goodness.

REFLECTION:

What is one example of God's goodness you have experienced recently?
Who can you share with about God's awesome work in your life?

"But you, Lord, are a compassionate and gracious God,
slow to anger, abounding in love and faithfulness."
~ Psalm 86:15

Christine M. Fisher

62

No One Walks Alone

While witnessing a basic military training graduation ceremony, two tenets of the Soldier's Creed they recited struck me as applicable to our civilian lives.

> I am a warrior and member of a team.
> I will never leave a fallen comrade.

It warmed my heart to learn of people God had placed in my daughter's path so she could experience the truth of those tenets.

The soldiers in training are given two pairs of boots. One woman opted to keep only one pair and gave the other pair to my daughter since hers were too small, which caused open wounds on her heels—she could barely walk. This soldier in training exhibited working as a team member, helping someone in need.

The other story was from the last big physical endurance test before graduation, which is called The Forge. It is a 72-96 hour adventure that spans 45 miles outdoors in the elements while performing various testing in skills. My daughter recounted how there were two men, one that went ahead of her and the other behind her, who helped keep her focused and motivated to continue. She felt bad that the one behind her retreated often to stay with her, though he could have finished earlier. In effect, both gentlemen were willing to sacrifice themselves to live out the tenet of "never leaving a fallen comrade."

Doesn't God do those same things in our lives?

"Therefore go and make disciples of all nations, baptizing them
in the name of the Father and of the Son and of the Holy Spirit,
and teaching them to obey everything I have commanded you.
And surely I am with you always, to the very end of the age."
~ Matthew 28:19-20

We are disciples on Team Jesus. We are called to share the gospel with others, bringing them into a personal relationship with Jesus. He leads us, providing what we need at just the perfect time. Jesus assures us that He is always with us, even until the ends of the earth.

"The Lord is not slow in keeping his promise, as some understand
slowness. Instead he is patient with you, not wanting anyone
to perish, but everyone to come to repentance."
~ 2 Peter 3:9

The Lord does not want to leave anyone behind because He has great love for all of His creation. Often we wander from the fold, but He waits patiently for us to return. There is no greater love than that which the Father has for His children.

Reflect on your relationship with others that God has put in your path.
Are you emulating Team Jesus, sharing His goodness, with the groups you are a part of?
Are you present to support those who need someone to keep them going strong?

Be encouraged to…

share with someone what Jesus has done for you.
rest in the assurance that Jesus is with you.
not let someone walk alone.
reach out to a trusted person when you need some help.

Christine M. Fisher

REFLECTION:

How can you better reflect teamwork in an area of your life?
Who is God leading you to extend some assistance to during their trial?

> *"Look after each other so that none of you fails to receive*
> *the grace of God. Watch out that no poisonous root of*
> *bitterness grows up to trouble you, corrupting many."*
> ~ Hebrews 12:15 (NLT)

63

The Gift of People

"Pay attention to the people
God puts in your path
if you want to discern
what God is up to in your life."
~ Henri Nouwen

We can learn lessons from every person we share life with. Maybe they teach us something to help us grow spiritually or personally, or model patience or how to love our enemies.

A by-product of publishing books has been meeting people who have become spiritual family to me. I grow in faith as I learn people's stories and have had the privilege of accompanying some in the final months of their lives.

A few months after my first book was published, an usher at church brought a man to me, someone who lived a few hours away. He read about me in our diocesan newspaper and was excited to meet me. That day started a three-year friendship as we kept in touch via phone calls, at church, or by sharing a meal. He shared several of my books with others.

His life changed in April 2022 when he was diagnosed with a tumor on his voice box, which left him unable to eat or drink. He endured many treatments and received the miracle of being declared cancer-free, something the doctors did not expect. The last hurdle of being able to successfully stretch his esophagus so he could eat and drink again became impossible, which was disheartening. They found another non-cancerous growth that was blocking the way. He died in December 2023.

What did I see in his life that challenged me?

> He never complained about his situation.
> Despite not being able to eat or drink, he was always willing to go out with the guys or us just to socialize.
> He was always thankful for all the good things in his life.
> He faced the challenges one step at a time.
> He believed and shared how so many others are worse off than he is.

> *Uncle Pete,*
> *Thanks for blessing my life and faith journey. You have been a treasure to know and love for three years, and you will forever hold a special place deep in my heart. God and I love you.*

Thirteen months after that article when I was on a pilgrimage to the Holy Land, a lady in the group introduced herself and said that because of that article, she was receiving my weekly reflections. I brought a book to her room and talked with her and her roommate for over an hour, sharing our faith stories. We still get together every few months despite living a few hours apart.

> *Marianne,*
> *Thank you for stepping out in faith to receive a stranger's weekly reflections. It filled my heart with joy learning about some of your faith journey and Jeanne's while on the pilgrimage in the Holy Land. Thanks for your sweet, caring spirit, which challenges me to be friendlier.*

One young man I did not connect with directly, but his mom gave him a book. He was about eight years old when he was in a religion class that I taught. He was the nicest, kindest boy even then, and I admired his family. Around the time of my first book, he was diagnosed with a brain tumor at the age of 37. He made good strides battling the cancer at first, but the Lord called him home a year later. He, his mom, his wife, and three young children remained strong in faith throughout it.

> *James,*
> *Thank you for being the most Christ-like student in my class who taught me to always be kind and loving. Your unwavering faith throughout your illness inspires me to have deeper faith, too.*

I awkwardly shared a book with a man at church. He emailed me a day later to thank me for the book and to share some of his story. We became spiritual friends and kept in contact for six months before he became ill. He attended my second book launch despite being ill. He died less than fourteen months after meeting him. My life was enriched by knowing him, and as a result of going to his funeral, I met and visited his mom for three years before she passed on.

> *Don,*
> *Thanks for the many spiritual discussions we had that helped challenge me to have more faith and trust. Seeing you at the Lord's table for the last time is forever etched in my memory and heart. I thoroughly enjoyed visiting with your mom and your brothers.*

Be encouraged to...

> pay attention to and be grateful for the people God is putting in your path.
> reflect on what God is doing in your life through the people you engage with.
> share with someone how you value the difference their faith has made in your life.

REFLECTION:

Who can you thank for the difference they make in your faith journey? What lesson from a friend do you need to grow in?

"So we praise God for the glorious grace he has poured out on us who belong to his dear Son."
~ Ephesians 1:6 (NLT)

64

One Bite at a Time

At a special service at our church, I saw a man I had given my second book to, and I asked if he was interested in my latest, *God's Compassion Illuminated*. He was excited to have it, saying he enjoys reading my reflections.

When I share this book with people, I mention that there is a section on the Holy Land. It often leads to conversation about it, and it's always interesting to learn of others who have experienced the pilgrimage or want to.

This man falls into the "hope to visit there some time" category. He also expressed interest in doing the 500-mile Camino de Santiago pilgrimage someday when he can afford enough time off of work. Pilgrims who embark on this journey usually walk routes that take them through Spain, France, and Portugal. The final destination is where James, the apostle, is believed to be buried. I shared how I, too, would love to do a portion of the pilgrimage someday, figuring I would never be able to tackle the 500-mile totality of it.

Right then, with serious eyes, leaning toward me, he says, *"How do you eat an elephant?"* I should have known the answer, but I said, *"I don't know. How?"* Obviously, he said, *"One bite at a time!"* After we finished talking and I started driving away, I burst out laughing and smiling, thinking about the wisdom he shared. Yes, what great truth and encouragement for me to reflect on. Five simple words that are so powerful.

Christine M. Fisher

Is there something in your life that seems overwhelming?

Do you have an unfulfilled dream you don't think you can make happen?

Is there something that seems impossible that God is calling you to?

"The Lord directs the steps of the godly. He
delights in every detail of their lives."
~ Psalm 37:23 (NLT)

Each day of our lives is made up of a series of steps. In reality, life is lived one step at a time. With each step, God delights in us and is always there to guide us. God knows the whole of our journey because He is sovereign. Our task is to trust Him with each step we take.

"Your word is a lamp to guide my feet and a light for my path."
~ Psalm 119:105 (NLT)

God guides each footstep we take on this journey. A lamp allows us to see one step at a time on the pathway. His Word is the light that illumines our path, showing us the way to go. We do not need to fear, knowing we are never alone.

Be encouraged to…

step out in faith to challenge yourself.
know God is directing you step by step.
know God cares about every detail of your life.
let God's Word illuminate your path, one step at a time.
take only one step at a time.
grin when you consider how you eat an elephant!

REFLECTION:

What is God calling you to step out in faith to do?
When did you see God directing your path?

"You then, my son, be strong in the grace that is in Christ Jesus."
~ 2 Timothy 2:1

65

Embraced in Love

Just as Jesus lived His life in unity with God and exemplified glorifying God in all He did, so we should as well. Jesus accepted people where they were, loving them and wanting them to come to know God. He inspired people to go deeper and change as they learned more about God. Accepting people brings praise to God as we try to influence them by sharing Christ.

> *"May the God who gives endurance and encouragement give you*
> *the same attitude of mind toward each other that Christ Jesus*
> *had, so that with one mind and one voice you may glorify the God*
> *and Father of our Lord Jesus Christ. Accept one another, then,*
> *just as Christ accepted you, in order to bring praise to God."*
> ~ Romans 15:5-7

The NICU is one of my holy places where I encounter God's presence, peace, and joy while snuggling, soothing, and loving babies. As often happens in our ministries, we receive much more than we give, which is what I experience in the NICU.

Here are two days of ministering in the NICU that I want us to reflect on.

When I was at the NICU that first day, it was so good to be back with some of the "pre-Covid" nurses who always welcome me with open arms and cheerful smiles. It is a sense of family and community, as we are all there because of our love for these little ones and one another. Though we are from different walks of life with different struggles and life events, we are one in our love and concern for the little ones.

The second day, a little girl that I held for most of my time stole my heart. As soon as I held her, all I could think of was how truly angelic she looked and how precious she was.

> *"Keep on loving one another as brothers and sisters. Do not forget to*
> *show hospitality to strangers, for by so doing some people have shown*
> *hospitality to angels without knowing it. Continue to remember*
> *those in prison as if you were together with them in prison, and*
> *those who are mistreated as if you yourselves were suffering."*
> ~ Hebrews 13:1-3

Our greatest task is to truly love one another. God's love for each one of us, no matter who we are or what we have done, is total unconditional love. We exist because of His great love. Jesus gave us the example of loving the adulteress, the leper, the marginalized, and the little children, just to name a few. Our human eyes may see just the external in people, but our hearts should see the value of each person that God created, no matter their circumstances. We are to remember and help those in need, whether we agree with their life choices or not.

As I gazed upon the beautiful, angelic face of this little girl, I saw the face of Jesus. Despite the unfortunate circumstances of her life, I was holding a miracle of life—a precious one made in God's image. Her lower arm bones were long and thin, as were her fingers. Two poses that she made added to her beauty. At one point, she held her arms in the shape of an X, with her lower arms in front of her chest. A nurse was nearby and said, *"She's sending the message of what she needs most: hugs and how important they are."* Yes, this little one needs to know how loved she is through the hugs and atten-tion she deserves. I stroked her head and face and prayed for her future, asking God to watch over her always. Her other arm position was so that her hands were tucked under her chin as she continued to look so angelic, peaceful, and content despite the inner turmoil she was experiencing.

Be encouraged to…

accept others as Christ did.
praise and glorify God for everyone you meet, even those who are
most different from you.
make others feel welcome.
extend hospitality to someone outside your normal circle of
influence.
pray for those in prison or suffering, whether it is their fault or not.
embrace and share God's love with others.

REFLECTION:

Who can you make feel welcome despite their different lifestyle?
Can you be challenged to see the face of Christ in the one who has done
something horrific?

> *"Grace, mercy, and peace, which come from God the*
> *Father and from Jesus Christ—the Son of the Father—will*
> *continue to be with us who live in truth and love."*
> *~* 2 John 1:3 (NLT)

66

Follow God's Way

Doesn't it often seem that we are constantly on the go, with our agendas dictated by what we believe we need to accomplish within a specific time frame? Perhaps you even make a list like I do to keep you on track. Don't we often have certain people we need to find and connect with even when attending church services?

While all those things are necessary, ponder how many times we pause and notice the...

person sitting alone in the last pew at church?
coworker who appears upset?
one at the grocery store who purposely avoids eye contact?
homeless person on the street in need?

"I will instruct you and teach you in the way you should
go; I will counsel you with my loving eye on you."
~ Psalm 32:8

Life is much better when we relinquish control of our days to God. He promises to lead the moments of our days because He knows how everything fits together to accomplish His will in and through our lives. God loves us so much that He is always ready to give us advice when we ask and listen to Him.

With this Scripture in mind, what if instead of just following our daily plans, we go about our days being open to God's connections and asking,

Christine M. Fisher

"God, who do You want me to see today?"

Maybe God wants to use you to...

> let that person in the last pew know they are valued.
> provide an understanding heart for the coworker to share.
> offer a friendly *"good morning"* to that person who tried to avoid eye contact.
> give some money to the homeless person for a meal.

What do we accomplish when we ask God who HE wants us to see today?

WE LIVE WITH INTENTIONALITY.

> *"Be very careful, then, how you live—not as unwise but as wise, making the most of every opportunity, because the days are evil. Therefore do not be foolish, but understand what the Lord's will is."*
> ~ Ephesians 5:15-17

When Jesus is our Lord and Savior, we have the privilege of knowing how He wants us to live. We want to follow His will as wise servants, helping those in need. Our time is spent seeking deeper communion with Jesus, being loved by Him, and then sharing that love with others. Our lives are not ours; we know our lives are about sharing Jesus.

WE CHOOSE TO DEPEND ON GOD.

> *"Yes, my soul, find rest in God; my hope comes from him. Truly he is my rock and my salvation; he is my fortress, I will not be shaken. My salvation and my honor depend on God; he is my mighty rock, my refuge."*
> ~ Psalm 62:5-7

As our faith in God grows, we see the goodness of God in everything that builds our trust in Him. Our roots grow deeper as we depend on Him to get us through, especially the difficult times. God is our rock and fortress. He is always there leading and guiding us.

WE LET GOD INTO OUR ORDINARY LIVES.

> *"He says, 'Be still, and know that I am God; I will be exalted*
> *among the nations, I will be exalted in the earth.' The Lord*
> *Almighty is with us; the God of Jacob is our fortress."*
> ~ Psalm 46:10-11

It is pivotal when we recognize that God is not just somewhere up in heaven, but rather He is a part of our everyday lives. We can experience His presence in the ordinary parts of our days and when we take a few minutes to be still and seek Him. If we are attuned, we will experience God in others, and they will experience Him in us.

Even if we are homebound and do not see people often, though hungering for interaction with others, the question, the prayer is still valid,

> *"God, who do You want me to see today?"*

God might be encouraging you to reach out to someone via a phone call, a text message, or an email. You might be the bright spot in their life that particular day.

Spoiler alert: Some days when you ask,

> *"God, who do You want me to see today?"*

you might be privileged to hear Him answer *"ME!"* Sometimes God wants us to slow down and spend quality time with Him. He longs to be our best friend and is always waiting for us to talk with Him, to share our deepest desires and happenings in our lives. That is God's goodness for us, His beloved children.

Be encouraged to…

consciously ask God throughout your day, *"God, who do You want me to see today?"*

live with intentionality, making the most of every opportunity that presents itself.

work on depending on God above all else.

experience God in the ordinary of life, whether you are with a room full of people or alone.

listen for God calling you to spend time with only Him.

REFLECTION:

Are you willing to be more open to God's connections?

Which of the three accomplishments above do you need to work on to let God in more?

"The Lord mocks the mockers but is gracious to the humble."
~ Proverbs 3:34 (NLT)

67

A Tribute

My heart is heavy since learning of another friend dying. It was quite a shock, as I had no idea—we lived almost three hours from each other. God, in His infinite orchestration, allowed me to be present at a gathering where one of her close friends was. She recognized me and shared that our mutual friend had a totally unexpected issue on Christmas Eve that resulted in her death a few days later. I ran across this quote that seems doubly appropriate to share.

> *"It is Christmas every time*
> *you let God love others through you…*
> *yes, it is Christmas every time*
> *you smile at your brother*
> *and offer him your hand."*
> ~ Mother Teresa

I interpret this quote as encouragement to make every day Christmas by the way we share even the simple kindnesses and joys to brighten people's days. We share the love of God with each other—and it definitely works both ways. It reminds me of the relationship my friend and I had.

> *"The memory of the righteous is a blessing, but*
> *the name of the wicked will rot."*
> ~ Proverbs 10:7 (ESV)

Christine M. Fisher

"Then I heard a voice from the heavenly realm, saying, 'Write this: Blessed are the dead—the ones dying in the Lord from now on.' 'Yes,' says the Holy Spirit, 'they will rest from their trouble, for their deeds will live on!'"
~ Revelation 14:13 (TPT)

It's difficult when we lose people. Scripture encourages us to keep their memory alive—that it is a blessing to recount the treasured memories that we have. It is comforting to know that the goodness of their lives continues to live on. As my pastor says, *"Gratitude is the antidote to grief."* So with a heart of gratitude for knowing my friend, to remember how she blessed me with God's love, and to share some of her good deeds, I write from my heart.

I met her at a retreat house where we did ministry for certain programs. I worked in the kitchen area, and she helped with the registration. We did not interact much in the beginning years, but she signed up to receive my weekly reflections. We bumped into each other a few years later where I learned she was growing in her faith through reading my first book because it was easy to understand and relate to.

Every now and then she would let me know when a certain reflection touched her even more, and she sent me a beautiful email that contained a few pictures of swans that made a heart shape. By then she had read my second book, remembering how God sends me reminders of His love with heart-shaped items.

One time she emailed to say that I wrote a reflection on her favorite song, "Angels Among Us," by Alabama. The song will always make me think of her and how she was an angel in my life.

Another day she emailed to say, "Just finished your latest book *(God's Compassion Illuminated)*. I got so much out of it. I really enjoy your writing." After publishing my fourth book, God inspired me to surprise her and mail her a copy of *God's Glory Manifested*. She sent me a thank-you note that I will always treasure. I noticed right away how she put a rainbow on the front of the card; to me, it symbolized the cover on my third book, and inside the note, she drew a heart, which represented my second book about God's love. Her message encouraged my spirit.

Only God could orchestrate us unexpectedly running into each other on September 20, 2024, at the retreat center for the final time. We embraced each other with a few hugs. I was there for a meeting and stayed for a luncheon. We ate together, enjoying each other's company. How blessed I am that I was prompted to get a picture with her and my latest book. It is the one and only picture we took. I love knowing she is now at home enjoying God's glory manifested at its finest.

When I shared with a friend, he reminded me to be grateful for the blessing of helping her grow in her faith as she journeyed home to the Lord. That is the positive that I will try to focus on, as I will miss hearing from and seeing her.

Three lessons that I learned from my friendship with this lady:

> There is beauty in letting others know how they impact our lives.
> A short email, text, or snail mail note is priceless.
> See the beauty of people's hearts—the God in them.

Be encouraged to…

> make every day Christmas Day.
> be loved by God through others.
> offer even the strangers a smile or friendly greeting.
> walk hand-in-hand with others.
> share God's love with all.
> keep the memories alive of those who are in eternity.

enjoy the present moment with others—you never know when it will be the last.

look for opportunities to help others grow in their faith.

REFLECTION:

Whose memory do you keep alive?
How can you let God love others through you, making it Christmas for someone?

"The Lord is gracious and righteous; our God is full of compassion."
~ Psalm 116:5

68

Who You Are

"Be who God meant you to be,
and you will set the world on fire."
~ St. Catherine Siena

The key to being who God meant us to be is based on who God says we are.

Who does God say you are?

"But you are a chosen people, a royal priesthood, a holy nation,
God's special possession, that you may declare the praises of him
who called you out of darkness into his wonderful light."
~ 1 Peter 2:9

Does your heart know that YOU are a most special possession of God's? He created you and loves you so much that He called you out of the darkness into His wonderful light. You are God's chosen one, and He considers you royalty.

"I praise you because I am fearfully and wonderfully made;
your works are wonderful, I know that full well."
~ Psalm 139:14

Does your heart know that YOU are fearfully and wonderfully made by God? He created you and fashioned you in your mother's womb. God made you unique; there is no other human being exactly like you. All of God's creations are wonderful and that includes you.

Christine M. Fisher

"For the Holy Spirit makes God's fatherhood real to us as he whispers into our innermost being, 'You are God's beloved child!' And since we are his true children, we qualify to share all his treasures, for indeed, we are heirs of God himself..."
~ Romans 8:16-17 (TPT)

Does your heart know that YOU are God's beloved child? God is your Father and the Spirit continually reminds you of being His beloved which needs to reach your heart. God lavishes you with signs of His love daily by sending you different treasures whether it is in the beauty of nature or providing people to journey with.

If you truly live as God's chosen one, knowing you are fearfully and wonderfully made and are His beloved child, wouldn't your life be on fire for God and the world? When you embrace the reality of your goodness in God's eyes, the fire of His love starts flickering.

How can we fan into flame that fire and set the world on fire?

By praying and studying Scripture.

"Devote yourselves to prayer, being watchful and thankful."
~ Colossians 4:2

"But as for you, continue in what you have learned and have become convinced of, because you know those from whom you learned it, and how from infancy you have known the Holy Scriptures, which are able to make you wise for salvation through faith in Christ Jesus."
~ 2 Timothy 3:14-15

God has given us two special ways to keep in constant contact with Him. Prayer is communication with God; a time to share our hearts in conversation sharing about the things happening in our lives and praying for those in need. When we read Scripture, we grow in wisdom as we learn more about God and the plan He has for living out our faith.

BY FOLLOWING THE TWO GREATEST COMMANDMENTS.

"'Teacher, which is the greatest commandment in the Law?' Jesus replied: 'Love the Lord your God with all your heart and with all your soul and with all your mind. This is the first and greatest commandment. And the second is like it: Love your neighbor as yourself. All the Law and the Prophets hang on these two commandments.'"
~ Matthew 22:36-40

Jesus came to show us how to love God above everything else and then how to love our neighbor. By living out the two greatest commandments, we are sharing God with all we encounter. God is love, and we, made in His image, are love too. What a privilege it is to emulate and share that love.

BY SHARING OUR UNIQUE GIFTS.

"Just as our bodies have many parts and each part has a special function, so it is with Christ's body. We are many parts of one body, and we all belong to each other. In his grace, God has given us different gifts for doing certain things well. So if God has given you the ability to prophesy, speak out with as much faith as God has given you. If your gift is serving others, serve them well. If you are a teacher, teach well. If your gift is to encourage others, be encouraging. If it is giving, give generously. If God has given you leadership ability, take the responsibility seriously. And if you have a gift for showing kindness to others, do it gladly. Don't just pretend to love others. Really love them. Hate what is wrong. Hold tightly to what is good."
~ Romans 12:4-9 (NLT)

We all have a unique toolbox of gifts that God has given us. As a valuable piece of the Body of Christ, we need to share our special gifts with the

Body. Our lives are the time we get to explore and grow in discovering and sharing our gifts to build others up.

Be encouraged to…

> embrace fully your identity as God's chosen, wonderfully made, and beloved child of God.
> set the world on fire through prayer, Scripture, loving all, and sharing your unique gifts.
> fan into a greater flame the fire of God's love.

REFLECTION:

What do you need to work on to embrace your identity in God?
How can you ignite a greater fire in the ordinary of your day?

> *"With great power the apostles continued to testify to the resurrection of the Lord Jesus. And God's grace was so powerfully at work in them all."*
> ~ Acts 4:33

69

Some Gave All

"Some gave all" came to mind as a friend shared about his flight from Florida to New York. They were delayed at takeoff, and once they landed and pulled up to the terminal gate, the flight attendant announced they had carried a fallen soldier home. The plane grew quiet, and there was total silence in the terminal despite the hundred people gathered by the windows to witness the casket of the fallen soldier being brought home. My friend's first thought was, "Suddenly what matters most hits you."

Is what matters most how much money we have?
Is the next fun event on our schedule what matters most?
Does it matter if our house is in tip-top shape?
Or is what matters most how we respect others, take time to listen to someone, or offer a lending hand to someone in physical need?

Memorial Day was only three days earlier as I wondered if the soldier died that day. We often hear the saying, *"All gave some, some gave all,"* referring to our military who put their lives on the line. This soldier indeed *"gave all."* At times like this, we all respect, honor, and have gratitude for those in the military. What sacrifices they and their families make to serve our country and protect the freedom our forefathers have passed on to us.

Thinking of this fallen soldier also made me think how Jesus too *"gave all"* for each one of us.

"Yet, Christ paid the full price to set us free from the curse of the law. He absorbed the curse completely as he became a curse in our place. For it is written: 'Everyone who is hung upon a tree is cursed.'

Christine M. Fisher

Jesus Christ dissolved the curse from our lives, so that in him all the
blessings of Abraham can be poured out upon gentiles. And now
through faith we receive the promised Holy Spirit who lives in us."
~ Galatians 3:13-14 (TPT)

Jesus gave His all for each one of us. He knew His sacrifice of dying on the cross was the only way to ensure our freedom from our sin—the only way we could spend eternity in heaven with God and Him. As hard as the suffering was, Jesus was willing to pay that price. What a gift it is that we now have the gift of the Holy Spirit, who lives in us and guides our path.

Do we have the same respect for Jesus as we do for our military?
Do we honor Jesus with reverence for being our Savior?
Do we take time to be still with Jesus?
Do our hearts overflow with gratitude for Jesus giving His all for us?

Be encouraged to...

reflect on what really matters in life.
thank a service member for their sacrifice.
share with Jesus the gratitude you have for His paying the price for your salvation.
show Jesus great respect for His sacrifice.

REFLECTION:

What do you need to focus on more in life?
How can you show honor to Jesus for His sacrifice?

"People of Zion, who live in Jerusalem, you will weep
no more. How gracious he will be when you cry for
help! As soon as he hears, he will answer you."
~ Isaiah 30:19

70

Intercession

My daughter embarked on joining the military in order to play in the military band. God's grace helped me experience great peace as she embarked on this path in life, knowing it is what she needs to do.

When she left for the ten weeks of basic training, I was in total awe of the intercession of so many people, most of whom have never met her. They were people whose lives intersected mine who were willing to intercede for a stranger. One lady in Wisconsin whom, the first time I talked to her on the phone, my daughter came up in conversation. From that very day, she has been faithfully praying for my daughter and my family as we stay in touch. On another occasion, there were pastors from Boston and India, the person at church who prayed with me the first time he heard, and the list goes on.

During basic training, when letters were a lifeline of encouragement to keep going, some of the strangers wrote letters to her. My daughter was sick throughout the whole ten weeks of basic training, which led to inflamed ribs that were painful. I know without a doubt it was all the intercession on her behalf that got her through it successfully and on schedule. My faith life has been strengthened through these prayers as well.

People continued praying through the next step, which was ten weeks of music school that still included the physical endurance part. She had to do extra work in both the music and physical endurance parts, but it all paid off as she successfully passed the necessary tests for both parts. Again, I have to credit the power of intercession, and my heart is filled with deep gratitude.

Christine M. Fisher

I was reminded of two Scripture stories.

"Then Esther sent this reply to Mordecai: 'Go, gather together all the Jews who are in Susa, and fast for me. Do not eat or drink for three days, night or day. I and my attendants will fast as you do. When this is done, I will go to the king, even though it is against the law. And if I perish, I perish.' So Mordecai went away and carried out all of Esther's instructions."
~ Esther 4:15-17

Queen Esther was undercover in the palace of King Xerxes. She invited the Jewish people to join in intercession and fast for three days and three nights—a significant number reminding me of Jesus being dead for the same amount of time before His resurrection. Queen Esther was going to be doing the same thing for the Jewish people. God intervened in the situation so that both Queen Esther and the Jewish people were saved.

"My prayer is not for them [the disciples] alone. I pray also for those who will believe in me through their message, that all of them may be one, Father, just as you are in me and I am in you. May they also be in us so that the world may believe that you have sent me. I have given them the glory that you gave me, that they may be one as we are one—I in them and you in me—so that they may be brought to complete unity. Then the world will know that you sent me and have loved them even as you have loved me. Father, I want those you have given me to be with me where I am, and to see my glory, the glory you have given me because you loved me before the creation of the world."
~ John 17:20-24

Jesus prayed prayers of intercession for His disciples AND each one of us. We are valued and loved. Jesus wants us to be united—in Him and with one another.

As the Body of Christ journeying in faith with one another, we are united in faith, though our lives may be different from each other. It is a joy to follow in Jesus' footsteps to intercede, love, and be unified.

Be encouraged to…

participate in the gift of intercession with those in need.
reflect on the specialness of Jesus praying for you.
give praise and glory to God for His goodness.
let people know you appreciate their faithful, prayerful support.

REFLECTION:

Is there a time when others came together for intercession on your behalf? Do you take time to intercede for others in need?

"When Apollos wanted to go to Achaia, the brothers and sisters
encouraged him and wrote to the disciples there to welcome him. When
he arrived, he was a great help to those who by grace had believed."
~ Acts 18:27

71

Celebrating the Gift of Life

As I get older, I have grown to appreciate the once-a-year day when we celebrate our birth.

I believe our lives are a gift
    from and to God and to one another,
        whom we have the privilege of sharing
            this journey of life with
                through God's perfect orchestrations.

It is most meaningful to spend a little time celebrating my life with those who have impacted my faith journey through "Celebrate Christine" gatherings. The greatest gift is hearing how my simple, ordinary life has touched others and maybe encouraged them in some way.

For the event, the first year I asked for the "present" of people sharing a note of encouragement or something they loved about me. This past year I asked for a special memory of us. Those truly mean the most and refresh my spirit. Isn't it important to share with people how their lives have impacted us and blessed us while we are still alive? Especially in the first year, reading what people wrote brought me to tears. I was graced with love reading about the goodness people see in me.

Birthdays make me reflect on how our lives…

    are an offering to God.

"So here's what I want you to do, God helping you: Take your everyday,
ordinary life—your sleeping, eating, going-to-work, and walking-
around life—and place it before God as an offering. Embracing
what God does for you is the best thing you can do for him."
~ Romans 12:1 (MSG)

Don't we often think God isn't found in the ordinary, mundane of our lives? The opposite is true. God is always working in our simple, ordinary lives. He sends us messages of His love and presence through the ordinary in life. All that we are and all that we do is our offering back to God for His goodness.

are sacred.

"Before I shaped you in the womb, I knew all about you. Before
you saw the light of day, I had holy plans for you: A prophet
to the nations—that's what I had in mind for you."
~ Jeremiah 1:5 (MSG)

Isn't it amazing to know that God knew us before we were even born? God, in His infinite wisdom, has a plan and purpose for each of our lives. We have the privilege of working with God to carry out His purposes as our lives reflect His glory.

impact every other life we meet.

"You are the light of the world. A city set on a hill cannot be
hidden. Nor do people light a lamp and put it under a basket,
but on a stand, and it gives light to all in the house. In the same
way, let your light shine before others, so that they may see your
good works and give glory to your Father who is in heaven."
~ Matthew 5:14-16 (ESV)

Because of God in us, we have the responsibility to shine His light into the lives of all we meet. Lights are made to dispel the darkness. The impact of our lives on each other should shine His radiance on all, which in turn gives more glory to God.

are filled with blessings from God.

"And God is able to bless you abundantly, so that in all things at all times, having all that you need, you will abound in every good work."
~ 2 Corinthians 9:8

God's grace in our lives provides all that we need to live fruitful lives. We can do good things for others because of God. He provides exactly what we need, whether spiritual or worldly, at the proper time for our good.

As I stop to reflect on each "Celebrate Christine" event, I am grateful for each person and the gift they are. It was fun to think of each person and remember how God orchestrated our intersecting paths. And, my dear reader, I feel the same about you. This quote sums it up perfectly:

"You make each day
a special day.
you know how,
by just your being you."
~ Fred Rogers

For each person reading these words, accept my heartfelt message to you,

"Thank you for being a part of my life which makes it a special day. You have impacted my life, and I am filled with joy because of the gift you are."

Be encouraged to...

offer the gift of you to God.
know your life is sacred.
shine God's light on those you encounter.
thank God for the blessings He sends every day.

REFLECTION:

Who can you bless by sharing the impact their life has had on yours?
What is one way you can shine God's light on someone this week?

*"The Lord is merciful and gracious, slow to anger
and abounding in steadfast love."*
~ Psalm 103:8 (ESV)

Christine M. Fisher

72

Angels

It was a lovely surprise to receive a link to a song a friend felt inspired to share. The lyrics and message speak to my heart and spirit.

The song is "Angels Among Us" by Alabama.

> "Oh, I believe there are angels among us
> Sent down to us from somewhere up above
> They come to you and me in our darkest hours
> To show us how to live, to teach us how to give
> To guide us with the light of love."[1]

Aren't there times in life when God sends angels to grace our lives?

Like…

the helpers during a natural disaster?
the friends who listen with both their ears and hearts?
those who protected us from danger?
the like-minded spiritual friends to encourage our faith journey?

*"Keep on loving each other as brothers and sisters. Don't forget
to show hospitality to strangers, for some who have done this
have entertained angels without realizing it! Remember those in
prison, as if you were there yourself. Remember also those being
mistreated, as if you felt their pain in your own bodies."*
~ Hebrews 13:1-3 (NLT)

Our greatest calling is to truly love one another. We are united in Christ. Do we reach out to the strangers who come into our lives, seeing how they enrich our lives as well as theirs? We all need those special angels as we remain open to God's orchestrations. Can you listen to others and empathize with their situation, whether they are in prison or need fairness in their lives? How can we reach out in love?

I was at a day retreat where I knew no one and jumped in to help pass out papers from the speaker. In doing so, a stranger asked about the shirt I was wearing that had a Christian message about love on it. This stranger was also one of four people who shared a story in her faith journey when the speaker engaged the audience. After she asked about my shirt, I had an inkling to share one of my books with her, and I definitely got confirmation after she shared. Leave it to God to place her right behind me when we were getting lunch, which led to us sitting together.

We had a lovely conversation, and she asked to hug me during that blessed encounter, which was special to both of us. Once again, two strangers shared stories of the Lord at work in their lives. We exchanged contact information as we live a few hours from each other. We talked and shared a few more hugs before we departed. She mentioned a few times that day that I was the angel that God sent her, and I felt the same about meeting her.

Two days later, she called to share some things that had touched her as she started reading my first book, *God's Presence Illuminated*. Our conversation lasted about two hours, which flew by as we both listened and shared, being able to relate perfectly to what the other was sharing. As only God can orchestrate, two days after that phone conversation, we enjoyed a three hour lunch. In our three encounters in less than a week, this stranger, this angel, has already inspired and encouraged my faith journey in countless ways.

Christine M. Fisher

Be encouraged, as the song reminds us, to see how God will use you to be an angel to…

show others how to live.
teach others how to give.
guide others with the light of love.
grace others with mercy in their time of need.

REFLECTION:

In what darkest hour did God send an angel to you?
When did someone view you as an angel of light in their life?

"James, Cephas and John, those esteemed as pillars, gave me and Barnabas the right hand of fellowship when they recognized the grace given to me…"
~ Galatians 2:9

73

Sea Turtle Lessons

We can learn lessons from so many of God's wonderful creations. I am in awe of God, the Creator, as I see numerous connections with His masterpieces.

What is applicable to us from a sea turtle's life?

Slow down.
> Make time for the beach.
>> Come out of your shell.
>>> Age gracefully.
>>>> Enjoy the view.

SLOW DOWN.

> *"Now as they went on their way, Jesus entered a village. And a woman named Martha welcomed him into her house. And she had a sister called Mary, who sat at the Lord's feet and listened to his teaching. But Martha was distracted with much serving. And she went up to him and said, 'Lord, do you not care that my sister has left me to serve alone? Tell her then to help me.' But the Lord answered her, 'Martha, Martha, you are anxious and troubled about many things, but one thing is necessary. Mary has chosen the good portion, which will not be taken away from her.'"*
> ~ Luke 10:38-42 (ESV)

It is important for us to slow down from life's demands. Like Martha, we can become distracted by the things that we have to do. Jesus reminds us

Christine M. Fisher

that we need to slow down to commune with Him and just be. When we are silent, we can better hear His voice leading and guiding our path.

Make time for the beach.

> *"You alone are the Lord. You made the heavens, even the highest heavens, and all their starry host, the earth and all that is on it, the seas and all that is in them. You give life to everything, and the multitudes of heaven worship you."*
> ~ Nehemiah 9:6

Looking around, can you see all the beauty in each creation? Making time for the beach can translate to seeing the magnificent splendor that surrounds us with both the inanimate creation and human beings that God made. We are so blessed to be able to praise and worship the Creator.

Come out of your shell.

> *"Be devoted to one another in love. Honor one another above yourselves. Never be lacking in zeal, but keep your spiritual fervor, serving the Lord. Be joyful in hope, patient in affliction, faithful in prayer. Share with the Lord's people who are in need. Practice hospitality. Bless those who persecute you; bless and do not curse. Rejoice with those who rejoice; mourn with those who mourn."*
> ~ Romans 12:10-15

While researching a little about sea turtles, I learned that they cannot retract their flippers or heads into their shells. I see this feature as an encouragement for us to continually be devoted to others in love. We should try to be aware of those in need, ready to give a helping hand whether in action, verbally, or in prayer. Sometimes it takes courage to step out in faith.

AGE GRACEFULLY.

"The righteous will flourish like a palm tree, they will grow like
a cedar of Lebanon; planted in the house of the Lord, they will
flourish in the courts of our God. They will still bear fruit in
old age, they will stay fresh and green, proclaiming, 'The Lord is
upright; he is my Rock, and there is no wickedness in him.'"
~ Psalm 92:12-15

As we age gracefully, we can grow in wisdom, understanding, and righteousness. If we keep Jesus at the center of our lives, though the numbers say we are older, we can continue to flourish and bear good fruit. Our circumstances change, but if our foundation is built on the Rock, Jesus, we know He will always guide and lead us.

ENJOY THE VIEW.

"Command those who are rich in this present world not to be
arrogant nor to put their hope in wealth, which is so uncertain, but
to put their hope in God, who richly provides us with everything
for our enjoyment. Command them to do good, to be rich in good
deeds, and to be generous and willing to share. In this way they will
lay up treasure for themselves as a firm foundation for the coming
age, so that they may take hold of the life that is truly life."
~ 1 Timothy 6:17-19

God has given us everything to help us enjoy the view. There is the natural world He formed to the people who journey with us to the opportunities we have to share the Light of Christ with others. Our view and the hope we have is based on God and His goodness. In helping and sharing with those in our path, we enjoy life to the fullest and are accumulating treasures in heaven.

Be encouraged to be like a sea turtle and…

make time to slow down a little each day.
revel in the beauty of creation while praising the Creator.
step out and take action to help others.
see how you can flourish and bear good fruit.
enjoy the view along your path.

REFLECTION:

Which sea turtle trait do you need to work on the most?
In what way are you most like a sea turtle?

"Rend your heart and not your garments. Return to the Lord
your God, for he is gracious and compassionate, slow to anger and
abounding in love, and he relents from sending calamity."
~ Joel 2:13

74

Stepping Stones

"Obstacles can either be
stumbling blocks or
stepping stones."

A friend, Greg Pedroza, shared that inspirational quote. His life example inspires me to want to be more resolute in my faith so that I, too, can live with confidence that, whatever my circumstances, God is to be glorified.

Greg, for over 43 years, has endured many physical obstacles. His latest obstacle started when he was admitted to the hospital for severe pneumonia and sepsis when he aspirated on food. Early intervention helped Greg get past those issues, but their effects will be with him the rest of his life. He is regaining the use of his voice, but he is unable to swallow properly, so he has a feeding tube to get nourishment. One of his biggest crosses now is missing his sense of taste. In addition, his legs have gotten weak after being in bed for six weeks.

Greg's life testifies to the truth of these thoughts:

"It's not what happens that counts... It's how you react.
Your mental attitude determines what you make of it,
either a stepping stone or stumbling block."
~ Bruce Lee

"Consider it pure joy, my brothers and sisters, whenever you face
trials of many kinds, because you know that the testing of your

faith produces perseverance. Let perseverance finish its work so
that you may be mature and complete, not lacking anything."
~ James 1:2-4

James is encouraging us to have a positive mental attitude through the trials that are a natural part of life in our fallen world. We live in an imperfect world with imperfect people, but God is still on the throne. He calls us to action to respond to our trials, regardless of size, by considering them opportunities for joy. The joy is not in the trials themselves, but in knowing that God works even in difficult circumstances.

I am always amazed at the positive attitude Greg focuses on, no matter what trial he is dealing with. I see how Greg, despite his current health crisis, maintains his wit and sense of humor, and brightens the days of his medical team as he reflects the joy of the Lord that is in him.

The only difference between a stumbling block and a stepping stone is how we approach it.

"Who shall separate us from the love of Christ? Shall trouble or hardship
or persecution or famine or nakedness or danger or sword? As it is written:
'For your sake we face death all day long; we are considered as sheep to be
slaughtered.' No, in all these things we are more than conquerors through
him who loved us. For I am convinced that neither death nor life, neither
angels nor demons, neither the present nor the future, nor any powers,
neither height nor depth, nor anything else in all creation, will be able
to separate us from the love of God that is in Christ Jesus our Lord."
~ Romans 8:35-39

If we use our trials as stepping stones in our faith, we are conquerors through God because of His love for us. We live knowing that nothing, whether seen or unseen, has more power than the love of God for His dear children. There will be times of difficulty, but we know that God is with us every step of the way, and this gives us strength.

I see how Greg lives with great faith and knows the depth of God's love for him. He shares God's love with everyone he meets, being upbeat, asking about others and their lives, and showing how much he cares about them. God is love, and Greg shares that same love with all.

When we replace "Why is this happening to me?" with "What is this trying to teach me?" everything shifts.

> *"Therefore, since we have been justified through faith, we have peace with God through our Lord Jesus Christ, through whom we have gained access by faith into this grace in which we now stand. And we boast in the hope of the glory of God. Not only so, but we also glory in our sufferings, because we know that suffering produces perseverance; perseverance, character; and character, hope. And hope does not put us to shame, because God's love has been poured out into our hearts through the Holy Spirit, who He has given us."*
> ~ Romans 5:1-5

When we look at our trials as lessons or stepping stones, we face them with peace, faith, and God's grace. We know that the lessons of perseverance, character, hope, and love are byproducts that ultimately draw us closer to God. Even Jesus endured great suffering with His death on a cross for our sakes, teaching Him the same lessons.

Greg's life, even when he was young, has always been about looking for the lessons that God is teaching him, especially through other people. He encourages others to reflect on how every person teaches us a lesson that we can apply and learn from.

Christine M. Fisher

Be encouraged when facing trials in your life to…

view them as opportunities for joy and know that God works in all circumstances.

know you can conquer them with God and His love.

see what lessons you can learn from them.

REFLECTION:

What stumbling block can you view as a stepping stone to growth?

Which of the three lessons do you need to work on the most?

"She [wisdom] will place on your head a graceful garland;
she will bestow on you a beautiful crown."
~ Proverbs 4:9 (ESV)

75

God Produces

God's purposes and what they produce in other's lives may not always be ours. I have seen how a simple gesture might have a different impact on someone's life than what we envisioned.

My friend, the church musical director, just completed twenty-five years of ministry. He doesn't like attention drawn to him, so there was no celebration. I felt this milestone needed something special and felt inspired to buy a crystal award that I was able to personalize for the occasion. It was meaningful to him, and it made him think, with gratitude, of all the people he has made music with through the years, as well as the pastors he has worked with.

He recently experienced some rough patches at his day job, and I was happy to see how God used the memento to be *"a soothing balm and provided me some healing and joy."* He appreciated being valued. Little did I know that following the inkling to celebrate him would produce that result in his life.

I recently attended a weekend retreat as well as a day retreat at two different places. I bring my books with me and try to follow the nudge to share with those who are on my path. God always seems to put "the" person in my path at the perfect time. I thought this one particular lady had left early, so I was pleasantly surprised when I saw her waiting for her ride in the lobby. I shared a book with her, and we talked for a few minutes. I was surprised when she said, *"I have wanted to write a book. You have inspired me to pursue this. Thank you for passing the torch."*

During a break at the day retreat, I took a few minutes to talk to the speaker and share a book with her. I was surprised to hear her say she has a website too and keeps getting phone messages from publishers saying they want to publish her book. She has no book yet but is wondering if the Lord is speaking to her. She said, *"Thank you for sharing this. I have been wondering if the Lord is calling me to write one. You have inspired me."*

I see the beauty in how the Lord used the simple act of following through on His inspiration to share with others in all three interactions. My obedience produced different results than I expected, showing me how the Lord's purposes prevail. It provided healing in one case and inspiration for the other two to pursue writing for His glory.

> *"Commit your actions to the Lord, and your plans will succeed. The Lord has made everything for his own purposes, even the wicked for a day of disaster."*
> ~ Proverbs 16:3-4 (NLT)

Isn't it comforting to know that if we commit ourselves to the Lord, we will succeed? We can stand by the truth of God's promises. All that God has made has a purpose.

> *"Many are the plans in a person's heart, but it is the Lord's purpose that prevails."*
> ~ Proverbs 19:21

As we go about life day by day, we make plans that are hopefully in accordance with God's purpose for us. Ultimately, God's purpose prevails as we live trusting in His ways.

Be encouraged to…

follow through on the nudges God provides.
reflect on the end result of encounters with others.
see what purpose God provides in your life.
see the impact of your actions on others.

REFLECTION:

What impact did a simple action on the part of someone else have on your life?
What nudge have you followed where you saw God produce a different result?

"We believe that we are all saved the same way, by
the undeserved grace of the Lord Jesus."
~ Acts 15:11 (NLT)

76

One

One person,
> one life,
>> one heart
>>> at a time!

Isn't it beautiful to see the Divine, God's hand, in our lives using one person, one life, one heart at a time to change one person, one life, and one heart at a time? Sometimes we are the one person, one life, and one heart that God uses to bless others, and sometimes our lives are the receivers of the special ways God uses one person, one life, and one heart at a time.

I received a website comment from someone who had recently signed up to receive my weekly reflections. *"I do agree that the simplest times in our lives are often the most meaningful to us, and though I've only been a follower of yours for a very short time, I have really enjoyed your messages. I am very grateful that I saw the article about you in The Tioga County Courier. I hope others decided to look you up after reading that article as well. God bless you!"*

Orchestrations of…

> one person,
> one life,
> one heart
> at a time.

A storyteller friend was unable to make his scheduled date for a library engagement and asked me if I would be willing to take his slot.

I finally accepted the invitation, fighting my feelings of inadequacy and asking for God's grace to help stretch myself.

God allowed only an audience of two people for my library share. One is a great supporter of my writing ministry, and the other was there to see the original speaker and did not know about the schedule change.

Both attendees decided to stay and listen to my talk.

My friend felt inspired to buy one of my books for the other person who stayed, enabling her to read some of my reflections.

An email friendship began with that person, and we were reunited at the eventual storytelling event for my good friend.

This new friend was inspired to write an article for a local newspaper about the storyteller and decided to include some information about my talk.

Reading about me in the newspaper is what led the person who wrote the comment on my reflection to sign up for my weekly website reflections.

We never know how God will use the simple, ordinary things we do in this life to further His kingdom.

I can't help but think about how often Jesus, in His interactions, touched one person, one life, and one heart at a time.

A few examples that you can feel free to read about are:

Jesus talks with the Samaritan woman found in John 4:1-26.

Jesus, a Jew, talked freely to a Samaritan woman which was forbidden. He knew this woman was living in sin

Christine M. Fisher

and needed His living water to change her life and her heart. We are led to believe that she changed her life after encountering Jesus at the well.

Jesus heals the man with a withered hand found in Mark 3:1-6.

On the Sabbath, when Jesus went into the synagogue, He saw a man with a withered hand. Jesus changed this man's life by healing him. This surprised the Pharisees, as they felt it would be unlawful to heal on the holy day. Jesus was very disappointed in their stubborn hearts.

Jesus and the adulterous woman found in John 8:1-11.

The Pharisees brought a woman caught in the act of adultery to Jesus, wondering what He would do with her. Jesus pointed out that we are all sinners and that she was no different from them. Jesus encouraged this woman to change her life because of His great love for her. He wants us all to repent and love as He does.

Be encouraged to…

stretch yourself to contact someone you have not heard from in a long time.
know that God uses you every day to build His kingdom on earth.
intentionally touch one person, one life, one heart at a time.

REFLECTION:

What is one way God used you to encourage one person, one life, one heart? Who needs you to encourage them today?

"And I am sure of this, that he who began a good work in you will bring it to completion at the day of Jesus Christ. It is right for me to feel this way about you all, because I hold you in my heart, for you are all partakers with me of grace, both in my imprisonment and in the defense and confirmation of the gospel."
~ Philippians 1:6-7 (ESV)

77

Teamwork

God made everything different yet with commonalities. A good case in point is to look at sports teams, individuals, and church communities.

SPORTS TEAMS

GOAL:	Work with one another to achieve a win.
CHOSEN:	Coaches pick the cream of the crop.
POSITION:	Each player usually has one specific position they excel at.
TEAM:	Every team member puts forth their best effort to succeed—sometimes sitting on the sidelines.

"You lazy fool, look at an ant. Watch it closely; let it teach you a thing or two. Nobody has to tell it what to do. All summer it stores up food; at harvest it stockpiles provisions."
~ Proverbs 6:6-8 (MSG)

Sports teams are like the ants that show us how to work well together and rely on each other to accomplish the goal. They keep going strong until the end. Each person knows their position and executes it to the best of their ability for the good of the team.

INDIVIDUALS

GOAL: Grow in a deeper and more intimate relationship with the Lord.

CHOSEN: By our Creator, God, to be His beloved and to bring His light to all.

POSITION: Each person has a unique calling through what we do, say, and accomplish daily to help fulfill God's mission for their life.

TEAM: The families God has placed us in and the people He puts in our path.

"O God, you are my God; earnestly I seek you; my soul thirsts for you; my flesh faints for you, as in a dry and weary land where there is no water. So I have looked upon you in the sanctuary, beholding your power and glory. Because your steadfast love is better than life, my lips will praise you. So I will bless you as long as I live; in your name I will lift up my hands."
~ Psalm 63:1-4 (ESV)

Our hearts have a longing that only God can fill; we are restless until we rest in God. When we seek Him, we are filled with His presence, love, and peace. His love is better than anything, and we can't help but praise and glorify Him.

CHURCH COMMUNITIES

GOAL: Share and spread God's presence, love, and compassion to a larger community.

CHOSEN: God has specifically recruited each of us to be a follower of Jesus.

POSITION: Sharing the unique spiritual gifts God has given to us.

TEAM: Members of the Body of Christ Team, which is
           the ultimate team—nobody sits on the sidelines.

"The human body has many parts, but the many parts make up one whole body. So it is with the body of Christ. Some of us are Jews, some are Gentiles, some are slaves, and some are free. But we have all been baptized into one body by one Spirit, and we all share the same Spirit. But our bodies have many parts, and God has put each part just where he wants it. How strange a body would be if it had only one part! Yes, there are many parts, but only one body. The eye can never say to the hand, 'I don't need you.' The head can't say to the feet, 'I don't need you.' All of you together are Christ's body, and each of you is a part of it."
~ 1 Corinthians 12:12-13, 18-21, 27 (NLT)

Paul wrote this Scripture to remind us of the unity there should be in the Body of Christ. Just as our human body has many parts that are all equally important and needed to work together properly, so it is with the Body of Christ. We are all a part of the Body of Christ and every person we see is an integral member of the Body. No member is more important than another; we are all equal.

Be encouraged to…

work on the goal of deepening your relationship with God.
let the sacredness of being God's beloved reach your heart.
praise God for your uniqueness.
be the best member you can be on the Body of Christ team.

REFLECTION:

Do you live truly believing you are God's beloved?
What is one way you serve others on the Body of Christ team?

"But to each one of us grace has been given as Christ apportioned it. Instead, speaking the truth in love, we will grow to become in every respect the mature body of him who is the head, that is, Christ. From him the whole body, joined and held together by every supporting ligament, grows and builds itself up in love, as each part does its work."
~ Ephesians 4:7, 15-16

78

Special Family

One of the definitions for the word "family" per Merriam-Webster.com that is quite fitting is: "a group of people united by certain convictions or a common affiliation: fellowship."

In 2021, at my local church, I awkwardly approached a man, a stranger, and shared my book. A day later, he emailed me and shared about the Holy Spirit in his life. That was the beginning of spiritual conversations for six months before he became ill and died a year after our first encounter.

I attended his funeral, which was a few hours away. At the luncheon after, I went over to his almost 90-year-old mom, introduced myself, and shared a book with her. She wanted to keep in touch and learn about the conversations her son and I had. That began our treasured friendship and visits.

How grateful I am for the last visit I had with her—the day before Mother's Day. We enjoyed a meal and, as always, enjoyed laughter and engaging conversation. I stopped at the cemetery where her son is buried on my way home. I thought it quite fitting that three birds appeared in the sky, disappeared for a few minutes, and appeared once more before I left. It reminded me of the Trinity.

Two weeks later, she passed away. But through my visits, I had the privilege of meeting her other two sons along with her oldest granddaughter. While at her memorial service, I was honored when they invited me to join the family prayer service at the funeral home before going to the church. Driving in the funeral procession, which was a first for me, made me think about being invited to process with Jesus on His way to Calvary.

Do we accept the invitation to be part of the biggest "family" of all time—God's family?

"Then Pilate turned Jesus over to them to be crucified. So they took Jesus away. Carrying the cross by himself, he went to the place called Place of the Skull (in Hebrew, Golgotha). There they nailed him to the cross. Two others were crucified with him, one on either side, with Jesus between them."
~ John 19:16-18 (NLT)

Have you envisioned walking with Jesus to the cross? He made that long, hard walk for us. Can you help Him carry the cross like Simon did? Do you let Jesus carry your crosses?

"Now all of us can come to the Father through the same Holy Spirit because of what Christ has done for us. So now you Gentiles are no longer strangers and foreigners. You are citizens along with all of God's holy people. You are members of God's family. Together, we are his house, built on the foundation of the apostles and the prophets. And the cornerstone is Christ Jesus himself."
~ Ephesians 2:18-20 (NLT)

It is a blessing when we come to accept the invitation to be part of God's family. We are united with Jesus and the Holy Spirit because of His sacrifice. We become part of the greatest "family" in all of history.

Be encouraged to…

reflect on the different families you are a part of.
journey with Jesus to Calvary.
be full of gratitude for being part of the most important family—God's family.

REFLECTION:

What unexpected "family" has God orchestrated in your life?
How have you helped Jesus carry His cross?

> *"Above all, love each other deeply, because love covers over a multitude*
> *of sins. Offer hospitality to one another without grumbling. Each*
> *of you should use whatever gift you have received to serve others,*
> *as faithful stewards of God's grace in its various forms."*
> ~ 1 Peter 4:8-10

79

Running Your Race

"Therefore, since we are surrounded by such a huge crowd of witnesses to the life of faith, let us strip off every weight that slows us down, especially the sin that so easily trips us up. And let us run with endurance the race God has set before us."
~ Hebrews 12:1 (NLT)

We are all running our own race as the Lord leads us to the finish line. Being surrounded by a huge crowd of witnesses, we are encouraged to run the race God has given us with endurance.

WHAT RACE ARE WE IN?

We aren't in a race to see how many tasks we can accomplish in a day, but rather we are running our race to live as faithful disciples, glorifying God with our lives, and sharing His great love with all.

As we run our race, we are surrounded by a crowd of faithful people, other runners, whose example can help us run our race even better. Some of these people have already gone on to be with the Lord, so we remember their example and the ways their lives of faith have impacted and left a lasting impression upon us.

Others are the witnesses we walk with daily, seeing how others are actively living out their faith, maybe dealing with great physical challenges, or maybe helping to support us through the tougher times. These people can help give us advice or point out when we might be starting to drift into a life of increased sin.

Christine M. Fisher

We are encouraged to run this race that God has given us until He calls us home. We never know when that will be, so we need to continually be faithful in following God and running with endurance.

WHEN DO WE GET TO THE FINISH LINE, AND WHAT IS THE FINAL PRIZE?

We each arrive at our finish line when the Lord calls us home. He was in control of when we were born and is also in control of when we die.

"For God so loved the world that he gave his one and only Son, that whoever believes in him shall not perish but have eternal life."
~ John 3:16

"But our citizenship is in heaven. And we eagerly await a Savior from there, the Lord Jesus Christ, who, by the power that enables him to bring everything under his control, will transform our lowly bodies so that they will be like his glorious body."
~ Philippians 3:20-21

The final prize for each of us is to obtain eternal life in heaven, where we will spend eternity rejoicing in God and Jesus' presence. There, we will also be reunited with our fellow runners who ran their races successfully.

HOW CAN WE RUN OUR RACE MORE SUCCESSFULLY?

Living as God's beloved and chosen ones.

"Put on then, as God's chosen ones, holy and beloved, compassionate hearts, kindness, humility, meekness, and patience."
~ Colossians 3:12 (ESV)

Have you taken it to heart that you are God's beloved child? We are most privileged to be God's children, His chosen and beloved ones, made in His image.

Using the unique toolbox of gifts God has given us.

Each one of us is born with our own unique toolbox of gifts that God, the foreman of our lives, has given us. We are given the task of discovering and using our unique gifts to bring glory to His kingdom. Maybe we have the gift of hospitality, sharing God's Word through teaching, or being generous with our time. At the end of our lives, we will give a reckoning to God for the way we have shared our gifts. It is important to not let fear get in the way of sharing our gifts. Our task is to be faithful in sharing, and God will produce the fruit in our lives.

Doing small things with great love.

Mother Teresa said, *"There are no great things, only small things with great love."*

We don't need to do big and lofty things as we go about our daily lives. What matters in the Kingdom of Heaven is living with a heart full of love as we go about our lives. We are encouraged to stand firm in our faith, be strong, and share God's love.

How Can We Train Better To Endure For The Duration Of Our Race?

> Have an accountability person or two that can keep you on the right track.
> Read Scripture daily to see how God is guiding you and keeping you on track with running your race.
> Take time to be still with God and stay tethered to Him to hear Him speak in the stillness.
> Strip away fear and let your faith be greater than your fear. Faith helps us grow, but fear paralyzes us.

Christine M. Fisher

Meet with other faithful runners in this race to encourage one another and share prayers.

Be encouraged to…

keep running your race faithfully.
keep your eyes on the prize of eternal life.
remember how a runner who has gone on to be with the Lord impacted your life.

REFLECTION:

What is one thing you can start doing to help run your race more successfully?
What is one action you can take to train better to run your race with endurance?

"By the grace God has given me, I laid a foundation as a wise builder, and someone else is building on it. But each one should build with care."
~ 1 Corinthians 3:10

80

Intentionality

A friend said,

> "Write about good friends being intentional, and investing in one another, and following through on plans so things do not stay stuck in the group chat."

A Google search for the definition of "intentionality" per Oxford Languages is: "the fact of being deliberate or purposive."

Isn't it important to live with intentionality? And isn't it equally important to live by investing in others?

The proper order of intentionality and investing is to be...

with our relationship with God first
and with others second.

When we live with intentionality, we are deliberate and purposeful about our goals and choices. We make an effort to live with purpose investing in others. As Christians, we want our actions, thoughts, and activities to reflect our goals of living life by honoring God and reflecting Jesus.

> "Seek the Kingdom of God above all else, and live righteously,
> and he will give you everything you need."
> ~ Matthew 6:33 (NLT)

How can we be intentional and invest in our relationship with God?

Through reading Scripture often, if not daily.
Taking time daily to be still with the Lord.
Taking time to pray and seek God's will.
Attending meaningful church services.
Singing songs of praise.
Taking time to share our experiences with other believers.

"And let us consider how we may spur one another on toward love and good deeds, not giving up meeting together, as some are in the habit of doing, but encouraging one another—and all the more as you see the Day approaching."
~ Hebrews 10:24-25

We live with intentionality and investing in our relationships with others when we...

take time to visit a shut-in regularly.
schedule time for coffee with a friend.
buy flowers for a friend to brighten their day.
attend a musical that a friend is participating in.
go meet our child when they have an hour of spare time.
check in routinely with a friend or relative to show you care.

What are some benefits of living with intentionality and investing in our relationship with God and good friends?

We draw closer to God and to our friends.
We think about others more, making the world a better place.
We build a community of believers.
We shine God's light in a sometimes dark world.
We are in obedience to the greatest of commandments: to love God and others above all else.

We have more peace and joy.

"The most important things are almost never urgent.
That's why it's essential that we schedule them."
~ Matthew Kelly

With our busy lives, remember to take time for the most important things: relationships and scheduling time with God. Impacting others is one of the greatest gifts. Make memories that last a lifetime.

Be encouraged to…

work on making your relationship with God the most important.
take one step to be intentional and invest in deepening your relationship with God.
make one group chat idea come to fruition with a friend.
schedule a get-together with someone so you can live a memory.

REFLECTION:

What is one way from the list above that you can be more intentional with your relationship with God?
Who is the Lord reminding you to reach out to?

"He has saved us and called us to a holy life—not because of
anything we have done but because of his own purpose and grace.
This grace was given us in Christ Jesus before the beginning of time."
~ 2 Timothy 1:9

81

Learning Lessons

Despite the vast number of people who currently live on this earth, who have lived before us, and who will live in the future, no two of us are alike. We look different, see and process things differently, and have unique experiences.

The beauty of this was brought to the forefront of my attention when I attended a talk from a friend, Greg. He focused on sharing how he consciously learns something from every person in his life.

When Greg was a child, he was encouraged to "run toward people," realizing the value of relationships. He grew up in a large extended family, and people were constantly around.

God has blessed me, especially these last few years, with expanding my world to include more people as I follow His path with this writing ministry. I have experienced the personal growth that comes from being more open to relationships, especially on a spiritual level.

Greg shared this Scripture that has brought even more meaning.

> *"You yourselves are all the endorsement we need. Your very lives are a*
> *letter that anyone can read by just looking at you. Christ himself wrote*
> *it—not with ink, but with God's living Spirit; not chiseled into stone,*
> *but carved into human lives—and we publish it. We couldn't be more*
> *sure of ourselves in this—that you, written by Christ himself for God,*
> *are our letter of recommendation. We wouldn't think of writing this kind*
> *of letter about ourselves. Only God can write such a letter. His letter*

authorizes us to help carry out this new plan of action. The plan wasn't
written out with ink on paper, with pages and pages of legal footnotes,
killing your spirit. It's written with Spirit on spirit, his life on our lives!"
~ 2 Corinthians 3:2-6 (MSG)

Paul, in writing to the Corinthians, shares that our lives are a love letter to God and the world. Because Christ sacrificed His life for us, we have the Spirit in us. The Spirit is alive in our hearts and helps us be the authors of our lives and our letters.

After listening to Greg share stories of the main lessons he has learned from different people, I was inspired to do the same. We can think about the lessons, good or bad, and see how they apply to our lives personally. Sometimes the lesson is something good that we can incorporate, and sometimes it is something we know we should not. It is important to remember not to let the past define our future. Let the past be the past. God will help us move forward.

A major lesson Greg has taught me is to focus on the "I can do," not the "I can't do." Greg has only limited function in his one hand, which has no tactile feeling, and he is not able to walk anymore. He has constant burning pain, except for a few hours when he is able to sleep. Yet he has the biggest, joy-filled smile that lets us know he cares for us and is ready to listen to what we have to say. He is able to spread joy and cheer by calling a list of people once a week to check in on them. He is continually praying for people throughout the day and mentoring different people, which are just a few of the ways he focuses on what he can do.

Here are some other lessons I have learned that have blessed my faith journey.

Relationships are important; include people to make them feel like family.

Christine M. Fisher

Reflect on how the Holy Spirit is always at work in our lives.
Always reach out to others, despite the dire circumstances you are experiencing.
We journey together with each other.
Engage others, showing them respect.
Put God's love into action by helping and serving.
Talk to the outcasts of society and let them know they matter.
Be a humble servant of God.
Cling to faith and one another during the hardships of life.
Make others feel valued and respected by listening with your heart.
Keep the attitude that everything is okay, despite everything going wrong.
To continually converse with God and listen to His voice.
Put your faith and trust in God, even if you're fighting for your life.
Extend a smile and have a good attitude to bring joy to others, despite your life circumstances.
It is good to share a quiet, deep faith as you sing praises to God.
To be cheerful and laugh every day, which will brighten others' lives.

It's important to share with others the lesson we have learned from them as our lives have a great impact on each other. We are each an important piece in the puzzle of life and the kingdom of God.

Be encouraged to…

make a list of people and the lessons you've learned from them.
ponder the letter you publish daily to God and others.
be flexible and open to how God wants to change you.
focus on what you can do versus what you can't do.
share with a few people the lesson that you see in their lives.

REFLECTION:

What lesson from someone's life has powerfully impacted yours?
What is one lesson you hope someone can learn from your life?

"And he gives grace generously. As the Scriptures say, 'God opposes the proud but gives grace to the humble.' Why, you do not even know what will happen tomorrow. What is your life? You are a mist that appears for a little while and then vanishes. Instead, you ought to say, 'If it is the Lord's will, we will live and do this or that.'"
~ James 4:6, 14-15

82

Unexpected Blessings

My husband and I decided to enjoy the last few days of summer with a trip to Rochester, NY. We randomly picked out two parks where he could bike and enjoy nature. The day before, I was visiting a friend whose son also stopped to visit. He mentioned a place I had never heard about that was an hour from where we were planning to go, so we decided to go there too.

As we were pulling into the first park, I thought about a friend I knew who lived in Rochester, which is a rather large city. I decided to text her, though she doesn't look at her phone very often, to see if we were close to where she lived. I thought it would be wonderful if we could connect for a bit, as I have only seen her at a retreat center. Much to my surprise and delight, within half an hour, she called to say we were at the park that is closest to where she lives—about five minutes away. She was not busy, so she came to meet me.

It was a hot day, so she suggested she could chauffer me around Rochester, showing me different sights that had an impact on her life. We drove by the house where she grew up in, her current home, churches, and schools, as well as some highlights of the area, like the waterfalls in the middle of downtown. She was excited to share the places with me, and I was honored. Before we knew it, three hours passed, as I had the privilege of learning more about the life of my special friend.

*"Sweet friendships refresh the soul and awaken our hearts
with joy, for good friends are like the anointing oil that
yields the fragrant incense of God's presence."*
~ Proverbs 27:9 (TPT)

How truly grateful I am for the people God has put in my path, especially
in the last few years. I have a spiritual family that indeed refreshes my
soul and fills my heart with joy. I experience God's presence through our
interactions and in their faces.

The unexpected blessing of finding out about a place called Chimney Bluff
Park, located on the shore of Lake Ontario, yielded a time of seeing God's
presence and beauty in nature.

*"For the Lord is the great God, the great King above all gods. In his
hand are the depths of the earth, and the mountain peaks belong to him.
The sea is his, for he made it, and his hands formed the dry land."*
~ Psalm 95:3-5

It's incredible to reflect on how God made everything and everyone. He
created everything we see in nature and in the animal kingdom. From the
sky to the dust on the ground, to the seas, to the mountains, to the tiniest
plant and even the smallest bug, God made them. We cannot escape His
presence and beauty.

God is a God of surprises. He has always been gracing people with unexpected blessings.

Consider the unexpected blessing of...

a young girl named Mary, who became the mother of Jesus, the
Savior of the world.

Abraham and Sarah who conceived a child when she was ninety years old.

each disciple, in the ordinary of their day, being called to follow Jesus.

God does great things when we aren't expecting them. This reminds me that He, not me, is always in control of our lives. In fact, a young man I was passing on the way out of church summed it up best when he said, *"Hello. It's nice to see you. Even these two second encounters are so meaningful in our lives."* This was only the second time I saw him as he lives out of state. I only know him because a friend shared one of my books with him. We were both filled with joy when we finally met to put a face with a name.

Be encouraged to…

be aware of the unexpected blessings God provides.

experience a blessing from nature.

remember that it is God who is ultimately in control.

REFLECTION:

What unexpected blessing did you see God orchestrate in your life? How have you been an unexpected blessing to someone?

> *"And this same God who takes care of me will supply*
> *all your needs from his glorious riches, which have been*
> *given to us in Christ Jesus. May the grace of the Lord Jesus*
> *Christ be with your spirit."*
> ~ Philippians 4:19, 23 (NLT)

Section 4

GOD'S GRACE MANIFESTED THROUGH THE FOOTSTEPS OF ST. PAUL

"For I am the least of the apostles and do not even deserve to be called an apostle, because I persecuted the church of God. But by the grace of God I am what I am, and his grace to me was not without effect. No, I worked harder than all of them—yet not I, but the grace of God that was with me."

~ 1 Corinthians 15:9-10

God's grace can work in everyone! Saul, whose name Jesus changed to Paul, at first persecuted many in the early church. Eventually, God's grace was manifested in Paul's life to the point of him being called to share the good news with the Gentiles, the non-Jewish people. What a radical change in his life.

God's grace in our lives helps us do things in Jesus' name that we never thought we could do. We might be called to step out of our comfort zone to share Jesus through speaking or serve those who are close to dying. God will provide His grace in whatever way we need if we have a willing heart.

In 2024 I had the privilege of walking in the footsteps of St. Paul retracing his second missionary journey in Greece and Turkey. I share some of my journey in this section. At the end of most of these reflections, I have included a web address where you can see more pictures, in full color, and more detail of the places.

God's grace manifested through the footsteps of St. Paul.

"Grace will follow us even when we are going the wrong way."
~ Ricky Maye

83

Help From Others

Is it easier for you
      to help others
         or
         to receive help from others?

"Meanwhile, Saul was still breathing out murderous threats against the Lord's disciples. He went to the high priest and asked him for letters to the synagogues in Damascus, so that if he found any there who belonged to the Way, whether men or women, he might take them as prisoners to Jerusalem. As he neared Damascus on his journey, suddenly a light from heaven flashed around him. He fell to the ground and heard a voice say to him, 'Saul, Saul, why do you persecute me?' 'Who are you, Lord?' Saul asked. 'I am Jesus, whom you are persecuting,' he replied. 'Now get up and go into the city, and you will be told what you must do.' The men traveling with Saul stood there speechless; they heard the sound but did not see anyone. Saul got up from the ground, but when he opened his eyes he could see nothing. So they led him by the hand into Damascus. For three days he was blind, and did not eat or drink anything."
~ Acts 9:1-9

Saul, whose name was later changed to Paul, had a powerful conversion that brought him to faith in Jesus. For years, he persecuted Jesus and His disciples. A bright light surrounded him, he conversed with Jesus and came to know who He was. Saul lost his eyesight for three days and relied on his friends to lead him to Damascus.

"In Damascus there was a disciple named Ananias. The Lord called to him in a vision, 'Ananias!' 'Yes, Lord,' he answered. The Lord told him, 'Go to the house of Judas on Straight Street and ask for a man from Tarsus named Saul, for he is praying. In a vision he has seen a man named Ananias come and place his hands on him to restore his sight.' 'Lord,' Ananias answered, 'I have heard many reports about this man and all the harm he has done to your holy people in Jerusalem. And he has come here with authority from the chief priests to arrest all who call on your name.' But the Lord said to Ananias, 'Go! This man is my chosen instrument to proclaim my name to the Gentiles and their kings and to the people of Israel. I will show him how much he must suffer for my name.' Then Ananias went to the house and entered it. Placing his hands on Saul, he said, 'Brother Saul, the Lord—Jesus, who appeared to you on the road as you were coming here— has sent me so that you may see again and be filled with the Holy Spirit.' Immediately, something like scales fell from Saul's eyes, and he could see again. He got up and was baptized, and after taking some food, he regained his strength. Saul spent several days with the disciples in Damascus. At once he began to preach in the synagogues that Jesus is the Son of God."
~ Acts 9:10-20

Saul's conversion story teaches us many lessons for our faith journey.

Jesus can reveal Himself in our lives at any time.
We can converse with Jesus like we do with our friends.
We can repent if we are going down the wrong path.
We journey with others.
We need to be open to the Lord's voice.
Jesus chooses unlikely people to build His kingdom.
The Holy Spirit is always available to give us power to spread the good news.
We all have a role to play in other people's lives.

How insightful to see that Saul had to be willing to receive help from others. We, too, need to gracefully accept help from people. We can provide healing in different forms for each other as we let the Christ in us shine on others.

Be encouraged to…

see how you can help open others' eyes see Jesus.
receive help from others, maybe even a stranger.
be vulnerable in faith, accepting guidance from others.
travel with other disciples.

REFLECTION:

Who has helped you to see Jesus?
Who can you help see and know Jesus?

"So in Christ we, though many, form one body, and each member belongs to all the others. We have different gifts, according to the grace given to each of us…"
~ Romans 12:5-6

84

Paul's Story

Paul's given name when he was born in AD 5 was Saul which is of Hebrew origin. He was an Israelite, from the tribe of Benjamin, born in Tarsus of Cilicia, which is considered part of Asia Minor, known as Turkey. Saul was considered a Roman citizen because his father was a Jewish Roman citizen.

At a young age, Saul lived in Jerusalem, studying the Hebrew Law with the Jewish scholar Gamaliel. He excelled in his studies and became a devout Pharisee. This is someone who believed a person must keep every one of the traditions of Judaism, as well as all the commandments. He was very legalistic.

Saul hated Christians and gave his approval of the first execution of a Christian leader, a man named Stephen.

"While they were stoning him, Stephen prayed, 'Lord Jesus, receive my spirit.' Then he fell on his knees and cried out, 'Lord, do not hold this sin against them.' When he had said this, he fell asleep. And Saul approved of their killing him. On that day a great persecution broke out against the church in Jerusalem, and all except the apostles were scattered throughout Judea and Samaria. Godly men buried Stephen and mourned deeply for him. But Saul began to destroy the church. Going from house to house, he dragged off both men and women and put them in prison."
~ Acts 7:59-8:3

Stephen, a man filled with the Holy Spirit, displayed courage and great faith as he was being stoned to death for his belief in Jesus. He, like Jesus, prayed for those who put him to death. Saul gave his approval of this tragic

Christine M. Fisher

death and began his mission to hurt, imprison, and even murder all those who followed Jesus.

From Saul's conversion story in the prior reflection, he went from being an arch-enemy of Christians to becoming the greatest Christian missionary. We learn that he became known as Paul. He is the author of more books of the Bible than anyone else and is also known as the "Apostle to the Gentiles."

"Saul, also known as Paul, was filled with the Holy Spirit, and he looked the sorcerer in the eye. Then he said, 'You son of the devil, full of every sort of deceit and fraud, and enemy of all that is good! Will you never stop perverting the true ways of the Lord?'"
~ Acts 13:9-10 (NLT)

Paul spent the rest of his life determined to spread the gospel to as many Gentiles and places as he could throughout Europe and Asia. He preached boldly, even in Jerusalem, and often encountered opposition and received death threats. He traveled on three main missionary journeys, another one to Rome and then his final journey after being released from two years of house arrest.

First missionary journey: (AD 47-49) Main route: Cyprus, Turkey— 1,400 miles
Second missionary journey: (AD 49-51) Main route: Syria, Turkey, Greece, Jerusalem—2,800 miles
Third missionary journey: (AD 52-57) Main route: Turkey, Greece, Lebanon, Israel—2,700 miles
Journey to Rome: (AD 57-62) Main route: Israel, Lebanon, Turkey, Crete, Malta, Sicily, Italy—2,250 miles
Other journeys: (AD 62-64) Main route: Macedonia, Troas, Miletus, Crete, Nicopolis, and back to Rome, where he was beheaded in AD 64, when Nero was emperor of Rome.

Books of the Bible that Paul authored to encourage the converts in his absence:

> Romans
> 1 & 2 Corinthians
> Galatians
> Ephesians
> Philippians
> Colossians
> 1 & 2 Thessalonians
> 1 & 2 Timothy
> Titus
> Philemon

Paul lived for 59 years and spent 27 years preaching the good news. Seventeen of those years he spent on his missionary journeys traveling throughout Europe and Asia. A major theme of Paul's preaching and his letters is about the grace of God. He realized that it was the free gift of God's grace that Jesus extended to him which radically changed his life.

> *"God saved you by his grace when you believed. And you can't take credit for this; it is a gift from God. Salvation is not a reward for the good things we have done, so none of us can boast about it."*
> ~ Ephesians 2:8-9 (NLT)

What a gift we have in receiving God's grace each moment of every day. It is a free gift; there is nothing we can do to earn it!

Be encouraged to…

> pray for those who persecute you.
> thank Jesus for how He has changed your life.
> rejoice in the way you share the gospel with others.
> see how God's grace is reflected throughout your day.

REFLECTION:

Is there someone who could benefit from learning your conversion story? What is the greatest grace that has impacted your life?

"But the free gift is not like the trespass. For if many died through one man's trespass, much more have the grace of God and the free gift by the grace of that one man Jesus Christ abounded for many."
~ Romans 5:15 (ESV)

https://www.hopetoinspireyou.com/2024/11/12/pauls-story/

85

Journeying with Paul to Philippi

Paul's secondary missionary journey took place AD 49-51, during which time Silas, Timothy, Priscilla and Aquila, and Luke accompanied him to some of the places. The journey began in Asia and was the first time the gospel message spread to Europe.

A major proponent of Paul's preaching and letters is God's grace. God's grace can be defined as manifestations of His presence, mercy, and goodness communicated through Jesus and the Holy Spirit—God sharing Himself. It is a free gift to each one of us; we are not able to earn it. Grace manifests itself as we become more aware of looking ever Godward to see His goodness. Sometimes we recognize God's grace in hindsight.

Paul began this adventure from the churches in Antioch, in Syria which borders Turkey, the same starting point as his first missionary journey.

> *"They [Paul and Barnabas] had such a sharp disagreement that they*
> *parted company. Barnabas took Mark and sailed for Cyprus, but Paul*
> *chose Silas and left, commended by the believers to the grace of the Lord.*
> *He went through Syria and Cilicia, strengthening the churches. Paul*
> *came to Derbe and then to Lystra, where a disciple named Timothy*
> *lived, whose mother was Jewish and a believer but whose father was*
> *a Greek. The believers at Lystra and Iconium spoke well of him."*
> ~ Acts 15:39-6:2

God's grace led Paul through Syria, Cilicia, Derbe, Lystra, and Iconium with Silas and Timothy. The church in Jerusalem gave them a letter to share with the churches in the areas that they visited. Paul and Silas had the support of the community of believers, well aware that God's grace would lead them.

> *"When they came to the border of Mysia, they tried to enter Bithynia,*
> *but the Spirit of Jesus would not allow them to. So they passed by*
> *Mysia and went down to Troas. During the night Paul had a vision*
> *of a man of Macedonia standing and begging him, 'Come over to*
> *Macedonia and help us.' After Paul had seen the vision, we got ready*
> *at once to leave for Macedonia, concluding that God had called us to*
> *preach the gospel to them. From Troas we put out to sea and sailed*
> *straight for Samothrace, and the next day we went on to Neapolis.*
> *From there we traveled to Philippi, a Roman colony and the leading*
> *city of that district of Macedonia. And we stayed there several days."*
> ~ Acts 16:7-12

God's grace is always working in our lives, and it inspires our faith when we are open to it. Because the Spirit would not allow Paul and his companions to preach about Jesus at Mysia, they went to Troas, a seaport on the west coast of Asia. There, the vision God gave Paul led him to know that God's grace was calling him to bring the news of Christ for the first time to people in Europe. They went from Troas to Neapolis, known today as Kavala, which was the principal port of Philippi.

> *"On the Sabbath we went outside the city gate to the river, where we*
> *expected to find a place of prayer. We sat down and began to speak to*
> *the women who had gathered there. One of those listening was a woman*
> *from the city of Thyatira named Lydia, a dealer in purple cloth. She*
> *was a worshiper of God. The Lord opened her heart to respond to Paul's*
> *message. When she and the members of her household were baptized,*
> *she invited us to her home. 'If you consider me a believer in the Lord,'*
> *she said, 'come and stay at my house.' And she persuaded us."*
> ~ Acts 16:13-15

Lydia is the first documented European convert to Christianity, thanks to God's grace leading Paul. She was already a worshiper of God, but her heart was open to receiving the saving power of salvation in Jesus. She and her household were baptized. Lydia began to serve in love by hosting Paul and his companions at her house.

While in Philippi, Paul and Silas were accused unjustly of advocating customs unlawful for Romans to accept and were brought before the magistrates.

"The crowd joined in the attack against Paul and Silas, and the magistrates ordered them to be stripped and beaten with rods. After they had been severely flogged, they were thrown into prison, and the jailer was commanded to guard them carefully. When he received these orders, he put them in the inner cell and fastened their feet in the stocks."
~ Acts 16:22-24

God's grace allowed Paul and Silas to endure the humiliation and beating they received as they stood firm in their faith. They knew God was with them and greater than the physical issues they were facing.

"About midnight Paul and Silas were praying and singing hymns to God, and the other prisoners were listening to them. Suddenly there was such a violent earthquake that the foundations of the prison were shaken. At once all the prison doors flew open, and everyone's chains came loose. The jailer woke up, and when he saw the prison doors open, he drew his sword and was about to kill himself because he thought the prisoners had escaped. But Paul shouted, 'Don't harm yourself! We are all here!'"
~ Acts 16:25-28

God's grace enabled Paul and Silas to praise God through praying and singing hymns despite their desperate situation of being in jail and bruised.

God's grace also provided an earthquake that allowed them to be free, but they acted with righteousness and did not run away.

> *"The jailer called for lights, rushed in and fell trembling before Paul and Silas. He then brought them out and asked, 'Sirs, what must I do to be saved?' They replied, 'Believe in the Lord Jesus, and you will be saved—you and your household.' Then they spoke the word of the Lord to him and to all the others in his house. At that hour of the night the jailer took them and washed their wounds; then immediately he and all his household were baptized. The jailer brought them into his house and set a meal before them; he was filled with joy because he had come to believe in God—he and his whole household."*
> ~ Acts 16:29-34

God's grace shining through Paul and Silas allowed for the jailer and his whole family to be granted salvation through Jesus, and they were all baptized. God's grace enabled the jailer to take care of the wounds of Paul and Silas and provided a good meal for them.

While reading the passages, I realized something that I hadn't noticed. Paul and Silas returned to jail that night!

> *"When it was daylight, the magistrates sent their officers to the jailer with the order: 'Release those men.' The jailer told Paul, 'The magistrates have ordered that you and Silas be released. Now you can leave. Go in peace.'"*
> ~ Acts 16:35-36

God's grace allowed Paul and Silas to do the right thing so that neither they nor the jailer would have any fear of recompense for wrongdoing. I find that a powerful act of God's grace.

*"After Paul and Silas came out of the prison, they went
to Lydia's house, where they met with the brothers and
sisters and encouraged them. Then they left."*
~ Acts 16:40

After all that Paul and Silas endured, God's grace provided encouragement to them as they returned to Lydia's house, where more brothers and sisters in Christ gathered. It shows the importance of the Christian community in our lives.

Be encouraged to…

> reflect on seeing God's grace leading you.
> deepen your commitment to love and serve Jesus.
> endure persecution with grace.
> live more righteously following God.

REFLECTION:

In what way have you been persecuted for your faith?
What grace from God have you received today?

*"In all my [Paul] prayers for all of you, I always pray with joy because of
your partnership in the gospel from the first day until now, being confident
of this, that he who began a good work in you will carry it on to completion
until the day of Christ Jesus. It is right for me to feel this way about all of
you, since I have you in my heart and, whether I am in chains or defending
and confirming the gospel, all of you share in God's grace with me. God
can testify how I long for all of you with the affection of Christ Jesus."*
~ Philippians 1:4-8

https://www.hopetoinspireyou.com/2024/11/19/journeying-with-paul-to-philippi/

86

Journeying with Paul to Thessalonica

"As was Paul's custom, he went to the synagogue service, and for three Sabbaths in a row he used the Scriptures to reason with the people. He explained the prophecies and proved that the Messiah must suffer and rise from the dead. He said, 'This Jesus I'm telling you about is the Messiah.' Some of the Jews who listened were persuaded and joined Paul and Silas, along with many God-fearing Greek men and quite a few prominent women."
~ Acts 17:2-4 (NLT)

We see God's grace in full force with Paul's willingness to preach about Jesus to the Jews. He wanted everyone to come to know Jesus personally and be assured of their eternal salvation. Paul's witness sowed the seeds for the birth of the Christian church in Thessalonica.

Scripture tells us that when Paul was still in Thessalonica, a riot broke out in the city because there were people who were jealous of Paul's preaching and the people that followed him.

"That very night the believers sent Paul and Silas to Berea. When they arrived there, they went to the Jewish synagogue. And the people of Berea were more open-minded than those in Thessalonica, and they listened eagerly to Paul's message. They searched the Scriptures day after day to see if Paul and Silas were teaching the truth. As a result, many Jews believed, as did many of the prominent Greek women and men."
~ Acts 17:10-12 (NLT)

Often we see how, when God's grace closes one door, another one opens. That is what we see with God leading the believers of Thessalonica to send Paul and Silas off to Berea. The people were more open to Paul's preaching about Jesus. God's grace inspired the believers to search the Scriptures to make sure they aligned.

Three steps from the synagogue where Paul preached in Berea

"But when some Jews in Thessalonica learned that Paul was preaching the word of God in Berea, they went there and stirred up trouble. The believers acted at once, sending Paul on to the coast, while Silas and Timothy remained behind. Those escorting Paul went with him all the way to Athens; then they returned to Berea with instructions for Silas and Timothy to hurry and join him. While Paul was waiting for them in Athens, he was deeply troubled by all the idols he saw everywhere in the city. He went

Christine M. Fisher

to the synagogue to reason with the Jews and the God-fearing Gentiles,
and he spoke daily in the public square to all who happened to be there."
~ Acts 17:13-17 (NLT)

Even when we preach the good news of Jesus, we can run into opposition, yet we see how God's grace provides. Paul, Silas, and Timothy were protected and kept safe. God used Paul's time alone in Athens for His grace to shine through. Paul noticed the idols that were everywhere and knew that the people were not following Jesus, so he tried to reason with both the Jews and Gentiles about this.

Because of what Paul saw in Athens, God's grace inspired him to share the following at a place called Areopagus (Mars Hill), which is a little northwest of the Acropolis where there were different temples for the Greek gods and goddesses.

"So Paul, standing before the council, addressed them as follows: 'Men
of Athens, I notice that you are very religious in every way for as I
was walking along I saw your many shrines. And one of your altars
had this inscription on it: "To an Unknown God." This God, whom
you worship without knowing, is the one I'm telling you about.

'He is the God who made the world and everything in it. Since he is Lord
of heaven and earth, he doesn't live in man-made temples, and human
hands can't serve his needs—for he has no needs. He himself gives life
and breath to everything, and he satisfies every need. From one man he
created all the nations throughout the whole earth. He decided beforehand
when they should rise and fall, and he determined their boundaries.

'His purpose was for the nations to seek after God and perhaps feel their
way toward him and find him—though he is not far from any one of us.
For in him we live and move and exist. As some of your own poets have

said, "We are his offspring." And since this is true, we shouldn't think of God as an idol designed by craftsmen from gold or silver or stone.

'God overlooked people's ignorance about these things in earlier times, but now he commands everyone everywhere to repent of their sins and turn to him. For he has set a day for judging the world with justice by the man he has appointed, and he proved to everyone who this is by raising him from the dead.'

"When they heard Paul speak about the resurrection of the dead, some laughed in contempt, but others said, 'We want to hear more about this later.' That ended Paul's discussion with them, but some joined him and became believers. Among them were Dionysius, a member of the council, a woman named Damaris, and others with them."
~ Acts 17:22-34 (NLT)

I have high respect for Paul, especially with this speech that God's grace enabled him to deliver to the council. His love and concern for these people was so strong that he risked everything to tell them how they needed THE true God. What a beautiful testimony to God's grace and greatness.

Be encouraged to...

> reflect on how you can share the good news.
> pay attention to how God is leading you.
> see how God's grace provides for you.
> ask God for courage to stand up for Him.

REFLECTION:

Whose life can you sow some seeds of faith into?
What idols are above God in your life?

"Now may our Lord Jesus Christ himself and God our Father, who loved us and by his grace gave us eternal comfort and a wonderful hope, comfort you and strengthen you in every good thing you do and say."
~ 2 Thessalonians 2:16-17 (NLT)

https://www.hopetoinspireyou.com/2024/11/26/journeying-with-paul-to-thessalonica/

87

Journeying with Paul to Corinth

The remains of the Temple of Apollo at Corinth

"Then Paul left Athens and went to Corinth. There he became acquainted with a Jew named Aquila, born in Pontus, who had recently arrived from Italy with his wife, Priscilla. They had left Italy when Claudius Caesar deported all Jews from Rome. Paul lived and worked with them, for they were tentmakers just as he was. Each Sabbath found Paul at the synagogue, trying to convince the Jews and Greeks alike. And after Silas and Timothy came down from Macedonia, Paul spent all his time preaching the word. He testified to the Jews that Jesus was the Messiah. But when they opposed and insulted him, Paul shook the dust from his clothes and said, 'Your blood is upon your own heads—I am innocent. From now on I will go preach to the Gentiles.'

Christine M. Fisher

"Then he left and went to the home of Titius Justus, a Gentile who worshiped God and lived next door to the synagogue. Crispus, the leader of the synagogue, and everyone in his household believed in the Lord. Many others in Corinth also heard Paul, became believers, and were baptized.

"One night the Lord spoke to Paul in a vision and told him, 'Don't be afraid! Speak out! Don't be silent! For I am with you, and no one will attack and harm you, for many people in this city belong to me.' So Paul stayed there for the next year and a half, teaching the word of God."
~ Acts 18:1-11 (NLT)

Just as in Paul's life, God's grace is always leading and guiding us. When he went to Corinth, God's grace provided community for Paul through strangers, Aquila and Priscilla, who arrived from Italy. They lived and worked together as tentmakers. We see Paul faithfully preaching in the Jewish synagogue, trying to convince both the Jews and Greeks to believe in Jesus, the Messiah. The people were not open to accepting His message and Paul knew it was time to move on, preaching more to the Gentiles instead. God's grace came to Paul in a vision one night, letting him know that God was with him and he would not be harmed. This enabled Paul to continue to preach faithfully in Corinth for a year and a half as more people came to believe in Jesus.

"I commend to you our sister Phoebe, who is a deacon in the church in Cenchrea. Welcome her in the Lord as one who is worthy of honor among God's people. Help her in whatever she needs, for she has been helpful to many, and especially to me."
~ Romans 16:1-2 (NLT)

Paul had great respect for Phoebe, a woman who served in ministry for the Christian church in Cenchrea. Paul entrusted Phoebe to travel to, deliver, and share a letter he wrote for the benefit of the early Christians in

Rome. God's grace accompanied Phoebe, and Paul wanted to make sure the Roman community treated her with grace too.

Be encouraged to...

> be a bridge that brings light into the darkness.
> extend gratitude for the community in your life.
> keep sharing the Lord with others and know He is protecting you.
> be trustworthy in your ministries.

REFLECTION:

Have you had to shake the dust from your clothes and share the gospel elsewhere?
Is there a "Phoebe" in your life that you can thank?

"Each one must give as he has decided in his heart, not reluctantly or under compulsion, for God loves a cheerful giver. And God is able to make all grace abound to you, so that having all sufficiency in all things at all times, you may abound in every good work. As it is written, 'He has distributed freely, he has given to the poor; his righteousness endures forever.'"
~ 2 Corinthians 9:7-9 (ESV)

https://www.hopetoinspireyou.com/2024/12/03/journeying-with-paul-to-corinth/

88

Journeying with Paul to Ephesus

Ephesus is located in Turkey, which is unique in that a small portion is located in Europe while the majority is in Asia. Ephesus, currently known as Kusadasi, is near the west coast of Asia and is the fourth largest city of the Roman Empire. Its spectacular Roman structures still possess glory two thousand years later. It was a major seaport in Paul's time for both the Greek world and then the Roman Empire.

"They arrived at Ephesus, where Paul left Priscilla and Aquila. He himself went into the synagogue and reasoned with the Jews. When they asked him to spend more time with them, he declined. But as he left, he promised, 'I will come back if it is God's will.' Then he set sail from Ephesus."
~ Acts 18:19-21

God's grace always gave Paul inspiration to preach and reason with the Jews and Gentiles wherever God led him. He knew he would return to Ephesus in the future if it was God's will, and he did during his third missionary journey. Priscilla and Aquila remained in Ephesus spreading the gospel.

One of the most impressive sites is the Great Theater of Ephesus, also called the Amphitheater of Ephesus. The riot of Ephesus took place in this theater over 2000 years ago.

"About that time there arose a great disturbance about the Way. A silversmith named Demetrius, who made silver shrines of Artemis, brought in a lot of business for the craftsmen there. He called them together, along with the workers in related trades, and said: 'You

know, my friends, that we receive a good income from this business. And you see and hear how this fellow Paul has convinced and led astray large numbers of people here in Ephesus and in practically the whole province of Asia. He says that gods made by human hands are no gods at all. There is danger not only that our trade will lose its good name, but also that the temple of the great goddess Artemis will be discredited; and the goddess herself, who is worshiped throughout the province of Asia and the world, will be robbed of her divine majesty.'

"When they heard this, they were furious and began shouting: 'Great is Artemis of the Ephesians!' Soon the whole city was in an uproar. The people seized Gaius and Aristarchus, Paul's traveling companions from Macedonia, and all of them rushed into the theater together. Paul wanted to appear before the crowd, but the disciples would not let him. Even some of the officials of the province, friends of Paul, sent him a message begging him not to venture into the theater."
~ Acts 19:23-31

"When the uproar had ended, Paul sent for the disciples and, after encouraging them, said goodbye and set out for Macedonia."
~ Acts 20:1

With Paul preaching about Jesus and there being only one God, a disturbance broke out as the silversmiths made their living by making silver shrines of Artemis, along with the other gods and goddesses they believed in. They knew their income would suffer if people believed in the one true God. Paul wanted to address those at the riot, but by God's grace he listened to his friends who begged him not to go. Shortly after this, Paul sent for his disciples and left Ephesus.

It was meaningful to proclaim Scripture while on this pilgrimage. I had the unique opportunity to read the following Scripture as we set sail from Ephesus.

"Some Jews who went around driving out evil spirits tried to invoke the name of the Lord Jesus over those who were demon-possessed. They would say, 'In the name of the Jesus whom Paul preaches, I command you to come out.' Seven sons of Sceva, a Jewish chief priest, were doing this. One day the evil spirit answered them, 'Jesus I know, and Paul I know about, but who are you?' Then the man who had the evil spirit jumped on them and overpowered them all. He gave them such a beating that they ran out of the house naked and bleeding.

"When this became known to the Jews and Greeks living in Ephesus, they were all seized with fear, and the name of the Lord Jesus was held in high honor. Many of those who believed now came and openly confessed what they had done. A number who had practiced sorcery brought their scrolls together and burned them publicly. When they calculated the value of the scrolls, the total came to fifty thousand drachmas. In this way the word of the Lord spread widely and grew in power."

~ Acts 19:13-20

While leaving Ephesus, we reflected on how Artemis, the Roman Empire, and even Ephesus have all fallen away, and the only reality still here is Jesus and the Spirit. They have stood the test of time from the beginning of the earth and are still going strong.

Be encouraged to…

> see who God entrusts to you.
> experience God's will directing your life.
> reflect on God guiding your footsteps.
> help spread the Word of the Lord.

REFLECTION:

When have you experienced God's grace guiding your footsteps?
How have you shared God's Word with someone this week?

*"For it is by grace you have been saved, through faith—and this is
not from yourselves, it is the gift of God—not by works, so that no
one can boast. For we are God's handiwork, created in Christ Jesus
to do good works, which God prepared in advance for us to do."*
~ Ephesians 2:8-10

https://www.hopetoinspireyou.com/2024/12/10/journeying-with-paul-to-ephesus/

89

The Last Day of Our Greece Journey

CRETE

The largest and most southerly of all the Greek Isles, our stop was only for a short time. I opted to walk along the coastline for a bit, where I discovered a fortress that translates to "Fort on the Sea." Paul had a connection to Crete—the opposite area from where we were.

We pick up this Scripture when Paul was being transported as a Roman prisoner from Caesarea to Rome, probably about 59 C.E.

> *"We made slow headway for many days and had difficulty arriving off Cnidus. When the wind did not allow us to hold our course, we sailed to the lee of Crete, opposite Salmone. We moved along the coast with difficulty and came to a place called Fair Havens [harbor on Crete], near the town of Lasea.*

> *"Much time had been lost, and sailing had already become dangerous because by now it was after the Day of Atonement. So Paul warned them, 'Men, I can see that our voyage is going to be disastrous and bring great loss to ship and cargo, and to our own lives also.' But the centurion, instead of listening to what Paul said, followed the advice of the pilot and of the owner of the ship. Since the harbor was unsuitable to winter in, the majority decided that we should sail on, hoping to reach Phoenix and winter there. This was a harbor in Crete, facing both southwest and northwest.*

"When a gentle south wind began to blow, they saw their opportunity; so they weighed anchor and sailed along the shore of Crete. Before very long, a wind of hurricane force, called the Northeaster, swept down from the island. The ship was caught by the storm and could not head into the wind; so we gave way to it and were driven along."

~ Acts 27:7-15

"After they had gone a long time without food, Paul stood up before them and said: 'Men, you should have taken my advice not to sail from Crete; then you would have spared yourselves this damage and loss. But now I urge you to keep up your courage, because not one of you will be lost; only the ship will be destroyed. Last night an angel of the God to whom I belong and whom I serve stood beside me and said, "Do not be afraid, Paul. You must stand trial before Caesar; and God has graciously given you the lives of all who sail with you." So keep up your courage, men, for I have faith in God that it will happen just as he told me. Nevertheless, we must run aground on some island.'"

~ Acts 27: 21-26

God's grace was at work protecting Paul's life and those on the ship despite the storm they encountered. Even while being a prisoner, Paul held onto his faith, encouraging those traveling with him since God said only their ship would be destroyed. Paul's life reminds us that suffering is part of our lives, but God's grace will always see us through.

PATMOS

Patmos is a small mountainous isle, about seven miles long and three miles wide. It has two narrow isthmuses that divide it into three parts. Patmos is most famous for being the island that Scriptures say the book of Revelation, the last book of the Bible, was written by a man named John.

Christine M. Fisher

"I, John, your brother and companion in the suffering and kingdom and patient endurance that are ours in Jesus, was on the island of Patmos because of the word of God and the testimony of Jesus. On the Lord's Day I was in the Spirit, and I heard behind me a loud voice like a trumpet, which said: 'Write on a scroll what you see and send it to the seven churches: to Ephesus, Smyrna, Pergamum, Thyatira, Sardis, Philadelphia and Laodicea.'"
~ Revelation 1:9-11

It was a sacred moment filled with grace to be where John was inspired by the Spirit to pen this sacred Scripture. It was special to have been at Ephesus, one of the seven churches John was told to write to. God's grace guides us.

Though brief, I hope you have enjoyed our journey through the footsteps of St. Paul. My prayer is that you have gained a greater appreciation for Paul and his call to spread the good news to the Gentiles. His story of redemption, his conversion story, is just like yours and mine! God shares abundantly His grace with us every moment.

Be encouraged to…

> soak up the beauty of the natural world God has made.
> spend a little time in solitude and prayer.
> see the ways God's grace is helping you through the difficult times.
> listen to the voice of the Spirit leading you.
> recognize God's grace throughout your days.

REFLECTION:

Where have you most experienced the beauty of nature?
What is one way you saw God's grace in your life today?

"But by the grace of God I am what I am, and his grace toward me was not in vain. On the contrary, I worked harder than any of them, though it was not I, but the grace of God that is with me. Whether then it was I or they, so we preach and so you believed."
~ 1 Corinthians 15:10-11 (ESV)

https://www.hopetoinspireyou.com/2025/01/07/the-last-day-of-our-greece-pilgrimage/

90

Moonlight

I had the privilege of sailing the same waters that Paul did on the Aegean Sea. I was the only one walking around in the dark of night while the moon lit up the water and seemed to keep spreading wider.

A few days later, I saw a devotion that mentioned how both the sun and the moon give light, but the moon merely reflects the sun's light and shines just a fraction of it into the world. I had never thought about how the moon has no light of its own; instead the moon's surface of craters, lava flows, and rocky debris reflects the brilliant sunlight.

Jesus is the light of the world, being like the sun in our lives. We, like Paul, are like the moon having no light of our own. By believing in Jesus and walking with the Spirit, we become witnesses and reflectors of Jesus' light to others sharing a fraction of the true light.

Be encouraged to…

> reflect on the spiritual lessons we learn from the moon and sun.
> thank God for your personal conversion story.
> pray your light will spread and shine on more people.
> ask for more opportunities to present in your life to reflect Jesus' light.

Whenever you look at the moon, may it be a reminder that its light is a fraction of the sun's light, as it is a witness to the light. May our lives be the same as we merely reflect the light of Jesus through our faith in Him and be reflectors of Christ's light to others through our love and actions.

REFLECTION:

What is one way you, like the moon, can reflect the light of Jesus in the darkness?

When have you encountered Jesus as a bright light in your spiritual journey?

> *"As a result of your ministry, they will give glory to God. For your generosity to them and to all believers will prove that you are obedient to the Good News of Christ. And they will pray for you with deep affection because of the overflowing grace God has given to you. Thank God for this gift too wonderful for words!"*
> ~ 2 Corinthians 9:13-15 (NLT)

https://www.hopetoinspireyou.com/2024/10/29/moonlight/

CONCLUSION

Thank you for taking time to read and reflect on the gift of God's grace. I hope these reflections have brought you to a deeper understanding of seeing God's grace manifested in your life. There are many facets to God's grace, but it is all because of His goodness and great love. May you continue to grow deeper in God's grace and be able to share it with others, drawing them into it too.

I will leave you with a reflection that I ran across and thought was a perfect ending.

> *"He giveth more grace when the burdens grow greater,*
> *He sendeth more strength when the labors increase;*
> *To added affliction He addeth His mercies,*
> *To multiplied trials His multiplied peace.*
> *When we have exhausted our store of endurance,*
> *When our strength has failed ere the day is half done,*
> *When we reach the end of our hoarded resources*
> *Our Father's full giving is only begun.*
> *His love has no limit, His grace has no measure,*
> *His power no boundary known unto men;*
> *For out of His infinite riches in Jesus*
> *He giveth and giveth and giveth again."*
> ~ Annie Johnson Flint

And a few nuggets of wisdom:

Grace remembered is grace renewed.
God's grace never lets us go.
Grace savored is grace deepened.
Grateful hearts see God's grace in every moment.

May we like Paul say:

"However, I consider my life worth nothing to me; my only aim
is to finish the race and complete the task the Lord Jesus has given
me—the task of testifying to the good news of God's grace."
~ Acts 20:24

ABOUT THE AUTHOR

Christine Fisher is a simple, ordinary gal, a child of God, a lover of Jesus, a daughter, wife and mother. She models her life after the ministry of Jesus Christ, serving and encouraging the lonely, the homeless, and the hurting. Through writing, Christine shares God's presence, goodness, and grace through the ordinary things in life. She enjoys spending quiet time in nature worshiping the Creator. Christine and her husband, Mark, live in upstate New York.

"Publish his glorious deeds among the nations.
Tell everyone about the amazing things he does."
~ 1 Chronicles 16:24 (NLT)
~ Psalm 96:3 (NLT)

"One generation commends your works to another; they tell of your
mighty acts. They speak of the glorious splendor of your majesty—and
I will meditate on your wonderful works. They tell of the power of your
awesome works—and I will proclaim your great deeds. They celebrate
your abundant goodness and joyfully sing of your righteousness."
~ Psalm 145:4-7

NOTES

1   Angels Among Us, written by Don Goodman and Becky Hobbs, 1993,
    Cheap Seats